The Bundled Doonesbury

A Pre-Millennial Anthology

by G.B. Trudeau

Andrews McMeel
Publishing
Kansas City

Doonesbury is distributed internationally by Universal Press Syndicate.

The Bundled Doonesbury copyright © 1998 by G.B. Trudeau. All rights reserved. Printed in the United States of America. CD-ROM manufactured in Israel. No part of this book may be used or reproduced in any manner whatsoever without written permission except in the case of reprints in the context of reviews. For information, write Andrews McMeel Publishing, an Andrews McMeel Universal company, 4520 Main Street, Kansas City, Missouri 64111.

www.andrewsmcmeel.com

98 99 00 01 02 BAM 10 9 8 7 6 5 4 3 2 1

ISBN: 0-8362-6752-4

Library of Congress Catalog Card Number: 98-85353

Doonesbury may be viewed on the Internet at:
www.uexpress.com and www.doonesbury.com

—— **ATTENTION: SCHOOLS AND BUSINESSES** ——

Andrews McMeel books are available at quantity discounts with bulk purchase for educational, business, or sales promotional use. For information, please write to: Special Sales Department, Andrews McMeel Publishing, 4520 Main Street, Kansas City, Missouri 64111.

"An Internet browser is a trivial piece of software."

—Bill Gates, December, 1995

UP AND AT 'EM, HONEY! WE'VE GOT AN ORPHANAGE TO GET READY!

>GASP!<

WHAT? WHAT'S WRONG?

SIR, YOU'VE... YOU'VE JOINED THE PRIESTHOOD!

GOOD EYE.

I DROVE YOU TO IT, DIDN'T I, SIR?

WHAT DO YOU CARE? I THOUGHT YOU PEOPLE WERE GODLESS.

©B Trudeau

...ANYWAY, BY LETTING THE OLDER KIDS WORK OFF THEIR KEEP, I FIGURE I CAN CLEAR $17,000 AN ORPHAN— AFTER TAXES!

AND WHERE EXACTLY DO I FIT INTO THIS PLAN, SIR?

WELL, INITIALLY, I FIGURED YOU'D BE DEN MOTHER...

Nothin' but Orphans Inc.

...BUT THEN I THOUGHT, HEY, SHE'S ASIAN—KNOWS HER NUMBERS! MIGHT AS WELL LET HER COOK THE BOOKS!

I BEG YOUR PARDON?

I'D DO IT, BUT MY MATH STINKS. I ALWAYS GET CAUGHT.

©B Trudeau

8

I CLEANED THE ATTIC, SIR, BUT I JUST DON'T SEE HOW YOU COULD FIT MORE THAN THREE BEDS UP THERE...

YOU ADD THAT TO FOUR IN THE GUEST ROOM, AND YOU'RE LOOKING AT A TOP CAPACITY OF SEVEN KIDS!

WAIT A MINUTE— WHAT ABOUT MY BEDROOM? THAT'S BIG ENOUGH FOR ANOTHER SIX COTS—EASY!

BUT WHERE WILL YOU STAY?

IN THE BAHAMAS. DON'T WORRY, I'LL BE FINE.

©B Trudeau

I MEASURED IT OUT, HONEY, AND I THINK WE CAN FIT TWO CRIBS IN THE CRAWL SPACE BEHIND THE FURNACE...

YOU CAN'T DO THAT, SIR.

OH NO? WHY NOT?

BECAUSE THE BABIES MIGHT ASPHYXIATE, OR THEIR CRIBS MIGHT CATCH FIRE AND THEY COULD BURN TO DEATH.

©B Trudeau

YOU'RE NOT GOING TO BE A BIG PAIN IN THE BUTT ABOUT MY ORPHANAGE, ARE YOU, HONEY?

>GASP!< YOU CAN SAY THAT WORD? AS A PRIEST?

AS MR. BUTTS RECALLS IT.

SO I'M JUST READING THE NEWSPAPER, OKAY?

DAILY BLAH

STATES OUT OF CONTROL!

SUDDENLY I SEE THE NEWS THAT **STATES** ARE PRESSING CLASS-ACTION SUITS AGAINST TOBACCO COMPANIES! I CAN SCARCELY BELIEVE MY **PEEPERS!**

FRANKLY, I'M STEAMED! THIS IS SUPPOSED TO BE A **CONSERVATIVE** ERA—WITH **LESS** INTERFERENCE FROM GOVERNMENT!

I DECIDE TO **DEMAND** AN EXPLANATION!

WHAT'S THE DEAL WITH ALL THE **LAWSUITS?**

I DON'T CONTROL THE COURTS.

YET.

MR. BUTTS RECALLS.

SO I ASK THE SPEAKER, "WHAT'S THE **DEAL?** I THOUGHT YOU PEOPLE WERE GOING TO **CONTAIN** PRODUCT LIABILITY!"

KEEP YOUR **SHIRT** ON!

...HE ADMONISHES ME.

WE'RE GETTING TO IT AS FAST AS WE CAN! THE PROBLEM IS THE LAWYERS—THEY **HATE** REFORM! TAKE THE FLORIDA SUIT, WHERE THE STATE IS TRYING TO RECOVER $1.4 BILLION IN MEDICAL COSTS...

KNOW HOW MUCH THE LAWYERS GET IF THEY WIN? $350 MILLION! **THAT'S** WHY THEY'RE TAKING ON TOBACCO!

YOU GUYS BETTER BE **READY!**

PANICKED, I ENROLL IN LAW SCHOOL!

BUT IT TURNS OUT TO BE **TOO BORING!**

AT FIRST I WORRY MYSELF **SICK** OVER THE FLORIDA CLASS-ACTION SUIT...

THEN SUDDENLY, IT **HITS** ME! THE SUIT IS FOR ONLY $1.4 BILLION! THE TOBACCO COMPANIES MAKE MORE THAN $50 BILLION IN THE U.S.!

SO EVEN IF WE **LOSE**, WE CAN HANDLE IT! NOW **THAT'S** CAUSE FOR CELEBRATION!

THEN I REMEMBER—THERE ARE 50 STATES!

I BUM MYSELF TOTALLY.

OKAY, SO I FLY DOWN TO FLORIDA TO SEE FOR **MYSELF** THESE "PATIENTS" WITH TOBACCO-RELATED ILLNESSES!

THIS PATIENT HAS EMPHYSEMA. EACH DAY HE'S IN THE HOSPITAL COSTS THE STATE $900. THAT'S WHY WE'RE SUING.

...CLAIMED THE ATTENDING DOCTOR!

LATER, I HAVE A DARK NIGHT OF THE SOUL...

I TAKE A LONG WALK...

I AGONIZE...

...I GET OVER IT!

HECK, I'M IN **FLORIDA!**

10

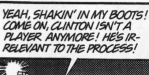

12

14

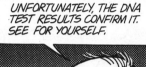

16

SIR, YOU'RE STILL GETTING KILLED OUT THERE FOR TAKING ON HATE RADIO...

I AM?

BUT I WASN'T TALKING ABOUT SPECIFIC RADIO SHOWS! I JUST MEANT PUBLIC DISCOURSE IN GENERAL...

BUT NOBODY BELIEVED THAT, SIR! AS LONG AS YOU'RE BEING PILLORIED ANYWAY, YOU MIGHT AS WELL TAKE CREDIT FOR WHAT WAS A VERY PRINCIPLED STAND!

HEY... IT WAS, WASN'T IT?

WELL, I SUPPOSE I COULD TEST THE WATERS...

HI, THIS IS BILL CLINTON CALLING!

I JUST WANTED TO CLARIFY MY POSITION ON HATE RADIO...

I DEPLORE IT! I THINK IT HAS CONTRIBUTED TO THE POISONOUS ANTI-GOVERNMENT MOOD IN THIS COUNTRY...

DO YOU THINK IT'S REALLY HIM?

DON'T YOU HAVE CALLER I.D.?

ANYWAY, I REALLY DID MEAN TO COME OUT AGAINST HATE RADIO. THERE'S BEEN SOME CONFUSION THERE.

MR. PRESIDENT, WHEN YOU SAY "HATE RADIO," ARE YOU REFERRING TO CONSERVATIVE, CALL-IN, TALK-RADIO SHOWS?

ABSOLUTELY, UNEQUIVOCALLY, YES!

HE SAYS YES.

IT CAN'T BE CLINTON!

... EXCEPT FOR RUSH LIMBAUGH, OLIVER NORTH, BOB GRANT, G. GORDON...

IT'S HIM.

... I'M ALSO NOT REFERRING TO THE BLANQUITA CULLUM SHOW!

BUT MR. PRESIDENT— YOU CLAIM THAT YOU'RE CONDEMNING HATE TALK RADIO...

...BUT YOU'VE JUST EXEMPTED EVERY MAJOR RIGHT-WING RADIO SHOW IN THE COUNTRY!

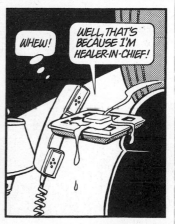

WHEW!

WELL, THAT'S BECAUSE I'M HEALER-IN-CHIEF!

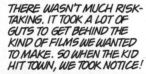

SID, WHY DID PHIL GRAMM GET INTO THE FILM BUSINESS?

WELL, I THINK HE HAD THE BUG...

ALSO, HE JUST LOVED SATIRE. HE FIRST GOT INTERESTED IN US WHEN HE SAW "TRUCK STOP WOMEN," OUR SPOOF POKING FUN AT INTERSTATE COMMERCE.

WHEN WE FINALLY GOT DOWN TO MAKING "WHITE HOUSE MADNESS," HE CALLED ME UP AND SAID, "IT'S GOT TO BE A SPOOF. I'M COMMITTED TO MAKING SPOOFS!"

SO THE FINAL PRODUCT?

TWO HOURS OF NON-STOP SPOOFING.

YOU SEE, YOU HAVE TO PUT "WHITE HOUSE MADNESS" IN POLITICAL CONTEXT...

GRAMM HAD BEEN A NIXON DEMOCRAT. HE FELT BETRAYED BY WATERGATE. WITH THIS SPOOF HE WAS GETTING BACK AT NIXON.

AND HE WAS DETERMINED TO GET IT RIGHT. AS A YOUNG PRODUCTION ASSISTANT, I TOOK A LOT OF CALLS FROM HIM. HE WAS OBSESSED WITH THE DETAILS!

PHIL THINKS TRICIA SHOULD WEAR A PINK DEMI-CUP.

TELL HIM TO STICK IT! THIS IS MY VISION!

THANKS FOR TALKING TO US, SID...

NOT AT ALL. WHEN DO YOU AIR?

TONIGHT. YOU DON'T HAVE A COPY OF "WHITE HOUSE MADNESS," DO YOU? WE'LL NEED A CLIP...

NO, I LOST MY COPY IN A MUD SLIDE.

KNOW WHERE WE CAN FIND ONE?

HMM...NOT REALLY. YOUR BEST BET IS THE PERSONAL LIBRARY OF SOME SPOOF COLLECTOR...

WELL, IF YOU THINK OF ANY...

TRY THE CLARENCE THOMAS COLLECTION! HIS CURATOR'S AN OLD PAL OF MINE!

MY ... LOOK AT THE BUILD ON THIS LITTLE FELLAH!

HA! HA! HA! HA! HA!

SERIOUSLY, I JUST WANT TO SAY I WOULDN'T BE UP HERE IF IT WEREN'T FOR THE ANGEL BEHIND "WHITE HOUSE MADNESS"...

...THE KING OF SEX SPOOFS— MR. PHIL GRAMM!

THANK YOU, CHERRIE! I'D JUST LIKE TO THANK THE ACADEMY...

WHAT'S THAT, DEAR?

24

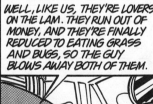

J.J., WHAT **ARE** YOU DOING, GIRLFRIEND?

YOU'RE FEELING GOOD ABOUT BEING A WOMAN, THAT'S WHAT! BEEN AROUND THE TRACK, SURE, BUT YOU STILL FILL OUT YOUR CUT-OFFS, GIRL! **WHEW!**

YOU CAN FEEL 50 PAIRS OF HUNGRY EYES, MEN WHO WANT ME, WHO WOULD GIVE UP **EVERY-THING** THEY HOLD DEAR FOR ME!

CALLING HUGH GRANT.

NAH. THEY MUST BE SHOOTING A COMMERCIAL.

THE ERSTWHILE HAUSFRAU, THE MOTHER OF ONE, CAUSES A STIR IN THE SLEEPY LITTLE TOWN. YOU CAN SEE IT IN THE EYES OF THE MEN...

"WHO IS THIS...THIS GODDESS?" THEY WHISPER. "WHERE DID SHE COME FROM?"

EXCUSE ME, MISS?

YES?

MISS, I'M AFRAID YOUR ACTIVITIES ARE IN VIOLATION OF TOWN ORDINANCES.

HOW'D IT GO?

ROMANCE IS DEAD.

ZEKE, I CAN'T **BELIEVE** I MADE SUCH A FOOL OF MY-SELF IN THAT TOWN!

HEY, C'MON, YOU WERE JUST HAVIN' FUN! DON'T BEAT YOUR-SELF UP!

I WAS ACTING LIKE A BIMBO, ZEKE!

YOU WERE NOT. YOU WERE ACT-ING LIKE SOME-ONE WHO'S BEEN STARVED FOR ATTENTION!

YOU DON'T **REALLY** WANT TO BE A BABE ANYMORE—YOU'VE DONE THAT! AND I WAS WITH YOU! NOW IT'S TIME TO MOVE INTO YOUR POST-BABE PERIOD. AND I'LL BE WITH YOU FOR THAT, TOO!

OH, ZEKE, YOU DO SAY THE MOST...

I MEAN, WHO **CARES** ABOUT ARM FLAB, MAN? YOU KNOW?

WHAT TIME WOULD IT BE IN NEW YORK RIGHT NOW, ZEKE?

WELL, LET'S SEE...IT'D BE ABOUT 9:15...

YOU STILL WORRYING ABOUT YOUR FAMILY, MAN?

A LITTLE. BUT IT'S BEEN NEARLY SIX WEEKS SINCE I SPLIT. I'M SURE MIKE'S STARTING TO GET IT TO-GETHER BY NOW...

I'M OFF TO DAY CAMP, DAD. DON'T FORGET TO BUY FOOD.

FOOD... OKAY... SEE YA...

26

HEAR THAT? THE UNEXPECTED KNOCK ON THE DOOR? IT CAN ONLY MEAN ONE THING—THE ONSET OF MIKE'S *SUMMER DAYDREAM!*

KNOCK! KNOCK!

KNOCK! KNOCK!

AND JUST IN TIME FROM THE LOOKS OF THINGS! COULD THIS BOY USE A BREAK FROM REALITY OR *WHAT?*

MIKE! DON'T KEEP YOUR MYSTERIOUS CALLER WAITING! HE'S HERE TO CHANGE YOUR LIFE!

RIGHT, AND THEN BREAK MY HEART WHEN I SNAP OUT OF IT. PASS.

UM...COULD I HAVE YOUR DAYDREAM, THEN?

KNOCK! KNOCK!

HELP YOURSELF. UNLESS IT'S A BABE.

MIKE'S ANNUAL *SUMMER DAYDREAM* IS UNDER WAY.

HI, DUDE!

BERNIE! YOU'RE THE MYSTERIOUS CALLER?

MICHAEL! JUST THE MAN I WAS LOOKING FOR!

MIKE, NO OFFENSE, BUT ANY DAYDREAM FEATURING BERNIE IS GONNA BE A SNOOZE...

I'D LIKE YOU TO HEAD UP MARKETING AT MY NEW SOFTWARE COMPANY—MOVE TO SEATTLE, TELECOMMUTE FROM YOUR HOME OVERLOOKING PUGET SOUND, WEAR FLANNEL SHIRTS, THE WHOLE NINE YARDS!

BOR-ING! DIDN'T I TELL YOU?

YOU'RE GOING TO START ME AT 300 G'S, AREN'T YOU? I CAN *TELL!*

IN MIKE'S SUMMERTIME FANTASY, OLD LABMATE BERNIE OFFERS HIM A DREAM JOB...

MIKE, I WANT YOU TO COME TO WORK AT MY NEW SOFTWARE COMPANY...

THE FINANCIAL PACKAGE IS ALL SPELLED OUT IN THIS ROLLING 5-YEAR CONTRACT—INCLUDING THE STOCK OPTIONS AND THE SIGNING BONUS!

GOOD GOD, BERNIE! YOU'RE INVITING ME TO JOIN THE... JOIN THE...

GO AHEAD, SAY IT!

THE UPPER-MIDDLE CLASS!

IT'S WHERE YOU BELONG, BIG GUY!

I DON'T GET IT, BERNIE! WHY ME?

YOU'RE QUALIFIED, AND AFTER YEARS OF UNDEREMPLOYMENT, YOU'RE HUNGRY!

ALSO, YOU'RE ROOTED, CENTERED. I VALUE THAT. THAT'S WHY I STILL WEAR THE BOW TIE AND POCKET PROTECTOR. IT REMINDS ME WHERE I CAME FROM.

EVEN THOUGH I JET AROUND THE COUNTRY SPEAKING TO BUSINESS LEADERS WHO HANG ON MY EVERY WORD, I STILL LOOK LIKE THE SAME AWKWARD, GEEKY MISFIT I WAS IN COLLEGE!

HEY... I WAS LIKE THAT, TOO! REMEMBER?

REMEMBER? HELL, MIKE, EVEN *I* SHUNNED YOU!

28

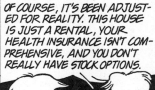

GOOD EVENING. TODAY THE ASSAULT ON FEDERAL SAFETY AND ENVIRONMENTAL REGULATIONS CONTINUED UNABATED...

ON THE SENATE FLOOR, DEMOCRATS FOUGHT A LOSING BATTLE AGAINST A MAJORITY COMMITTED TO THE WHOLESALE DISMANTLING OF PUBLIC SAFETY STANDARDS...

...WHILE IN THE CAUCUS ROOM, SENATOR BOB DOLE MET WITH THE BUSINESS LOBBY COMMUNITY TO SOLICIT THEIR "INPUT"...

OKAY, WHO'D LIKE TO RE-WRITE THE CLEAN AIR ACT?
RIGHT HERE, SENATOR!
I'LL TAKE A SHOT!
ME!
ME!

SENATOR DOLE INVITES INDUSTRY TO REWRITE ITS OWN REGULATIONS...
WHAT WE'RE DOING TODAY, OF COURSE, IS NOT WITHOUT POLITICAL RISK...

AFTER ALL, WE'RE ATTEMPTING TO GUT SAFETY AND ENVIRONMENTAL LAWS WITH PROVEN EFFECTIVENESS AND POPULARITY, LAWS THAT ACTUALLY WORKED...

BUT AT A TRAGIC COST TO OUR STOCKHOLDERS!
BAM!

I WAS GETTING TO THAT, JIM.
OH... SORRY, SENATOR... I'M A LITTLE DISORIENTED HERE.

LET ME JUST SAY AGAIN IT'S A PLEASURE TO BE WORKING ON REGULATORY REFORM WITH THE LOBBYIST COMMUNITY! IT'S A GREAT DAY FOR COST-BENEFIT ANALYSIS!

OKAY, LET'S TRY TO GET A CONSENSUS ON SOME FUNDAMENTALS. FIRST OF ALL, WHAT'S AN AMERICAN LIFE WORTH?

MEAT INDUSTRY?
SENATOR DOLE, WE PUT THAT FIGURE AT ABOUT $35.

REALLY? WE GOT IT PEGGED AT 12¢...
THAT'S WHAT I MEANT.

WHAT WE WANT TO DO, THEN, IS REQUIRE REGULATORY AGENCIES TO DO COST-BENEFIT ANALYSIS OF EVEN THEIR MOST EFFECTIVE RULES...

...AND NATURALLY, WE SEEK YOUR INPUT HERE.
ONE SUGGESTION, SENATOR...

IF YOU MAKE THE COST-BENEFIT REQUIREMENTS ONEROUS ENOUGH, THE AGENCIES WILL BE SO TIED UP TRYING TO DEFEND THEIR REGULATIONS, THEY'LL HAVE NO RESOURCES FOR ENFORCING THEM!

ACTUALLY, WE ALREADY THOUGHT OF THAT, PHIL.
EXCELLENT! CAN WE PROVIDE THE LANGUAGE?

30

BOB, LET ME SEE IF I UNDERSTAND YOUR REGULATORY REFORM DRAFT...

SAY, JUST SAY, I'M POLLUTING. WHAT IF THE FEDS DO ONE OF THESE COST-BENEFIT ANALYSES, AND I **STILL** HAVE TO CLEAN UP?

IN THAT CASE, YOU GO TO COURT! WE'VE MADE IT **MUCH** EASIER TO SUE THE GOVERNMENT!

AND WE'RE ALLOWED TO **CONTINUE** POLLUTING WHILE IT'S TIED UP IN COURT?

I'M TELLING YOU, JIM— THIS IS **REAL** REFORM!

WHEW. I GUESS! IT'S JUST HARD TO BELIEVE!

SENATOR DOLE, DO YOU THINK YOUR GUTTING OF THE HEALTH AND SAFETY LAWS WILL PLAY WELL IN THE UPCOMING PRESIDENTIAL RACE?

YES. I THINK THE AMERICAN PEOPLE FULLY SUPPORT REGULATORY RELIEF FOR INDUSTRY. THEY UNDERSTAND THAT BUSINESSES NEED TO BE HEALTHY, TOO.

I CERTAINLY DON'T THINK IT'S AN ISSUE THAT WILL COME BACK TO HAUNT ME, IF THAT'S WHAT YOU MEAN.

LATER...

LADIES AND GENTLEMEN, I GIVE YOU SENATOR BOB "E. COLI" DOLE!

HEY, MEN— WHAT'S UP?

WE'RE LOADING IN THE NEW WINDOWS 95 OPERATING SYSTEM, MIKE.

OH, YEAH? HOW'S IT LOOK?

DON'T KNOW YET. I'M STILL TRYING TO CLEAR ENOUGH MEMORY FOR IT...

Attention User: You call this capacity? Reboot when you're ready to play.

SON OF A... IT'S DISSING MY **HARD DRIVE!**

BACK OFF, HANK. DON'T MAKE IT LOSE FACE...

WHAT'S WRONG? WHY'S THE NEW WINDOWS BALKING?

IT'S GREEDY. IT'S HOLDING OUT FOR 16 MEGABYTES RAM...

...OTHERWISE IT RUNS APPLICATIONS AT A CRAWL. IT ALSO WANTS A FASTER MICROPROCESSOR AND 35 MEGABYTES ON THE HARD DRIVE...

...WITH 89 MORE FOR OFFICE PROGRAMS, AND... HEY... IT JUST TURNED ON THE PRINTER!

IT'S A COMPLETE LIST OF ITS DEMANDS!

GIVE NO QUARTER! HOLD IT TO ITS BOX SPECS!

HEY, HANK, DID YOU GET WINDOWS 95 LOADED IN YET?

YUP. TAKE A LOOK...

ICONS JUST LIKE APPLE'S, FILES AND FOLDERS JUST LIKE APPLE'S, TASK BARS, MENUS, TRASH FUNCTIONS— THE WHOLE APPLE DESKTOP ENVIRONMENT!

MAN... THEY CAN GET AWAY WITH THAT?

CHECK THE BACK OF THE BOX.

"THIS PRODUCT SUPPORTED BY 3,000 LAWYERS."

THAT'S ONE HELLUVA PLATFORM.

BERNIE, I DON'T GET IT—WHY ARE WE GOING WITH MICROSOFT IF WINDOWS 95 IS JUST ANOTHER APPLE RIP-OFF?

MIKE, WHO MAKES THE SOFTWARE THAT RUNS 80% OF THE WORLD'S P.C.'S?

MICROSOFT, OF COURSE.

AND DOES THE WORLD RUN ON COMPUTERS?

SURE.

SO WHO RULES THE WORLD?

≥ SIGH ≤ ...WHY DON'T WE JUST GIVE BILL GATES ALL THE MONEY NOW AND GET IT OVER WITH?

PRIDE.

THE THING IS, MIKE, IT DOESN'T REALLY MATTER WHAT YOU OR I THINK OF WINDOWS. WE DEVELOP SOFTWARE, AND WINDOWS RULES!

YOU GOTTA DISCOUNT ANY NEGATIVE BUZZ YOU HEAR. A LOT OF IT'S JEALOUSY. WHO WOULDN'T WANT TO BE SITTING WHERE GATES IS?

I MYSELF WOULD LOVE TO HAVE A STRANGLEHOLD ON A WHOLE INDUSTRY. I'VE OFTEN FANTASIZED ABOUT GETTING THAT FIRST PHONE CALL FROM THE JUSTICE DEPARTMENT!

YOU HAVE?

ABSOLUTELY. THAT'S WHEN YOU'VE ARRIVED!

HI, BABE!

DADSTER! SOMEONE DOWNLOADED A NEW SYSTEM INTO OUR COMPUTER TODAY!

THAT WOULD BE WINDOWS 95...

RIGHT. IT'S NOT BAD. IT'S GOT A COOL NEW GAME ON IT...

ONLY PROBLEM I NOTICED WAS THE P.C. SOMETIMES SLOWED DOWN WHEN I ASKED IT TO DO TWO THINGS AT ONCE...

THAT'S CALLED MULTI-TASKING, SQUIRT. YOU SEE...

OH, RIGHT. ANYWAY, I REWROTE THE CODE. IT'S OKAY NOW.

32

34

35

SURE IS QUIET IN THERE...

COULD ACTUAL STUDYING BE TAKING PLACE?

HISTORY PAPER TIME...

"Louisiana Purchase (1803): The purchase of the vast Louisiana Territory from France, initiated by Thomas Jefferson."

"The purchased area, which extended from the Mississippi to the Rocky Mountains, doubled the size of the United States."

The Louisiana Purchase in 1803 was the purchase of the vast Louisiana Territory from France at the initiation of Thomas Jefferson.

The area that was purchased extended from the Mississippi to the Rockies and doubled the size of the United States.

MY... WHAT A DRAMATIC IMPROVEMENT IN OUR WRITING.

THANKS.

TODAY PHIL GRAMM DISMISSED BOB DOLE'S WAR WOUND...

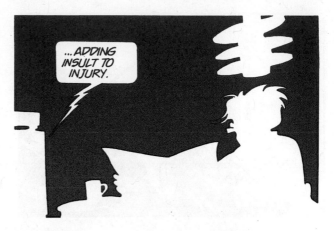

...ADDING INSULT TO INJURY.

HI, MY NAME'S BOB DOLE, AND I'D LIKE TO TALK TO YOU TONIGHT ABOUT MY OLD WAR WOUND.

YOU KNOW, THERE USED TO BE A TIME IN AMERICA WHEN HEROES WERE MODEST. A REAL WAR HERO ALWAYS SHRUGGED OFF HIS HEROICS. HE WAS JUST GRATEFUL TO BE ALIVE, HUMBLED BY GOD'S MERCY...

I MYSELF HAVE ALWAYS TRIED TO BEAR MY INJURY WITH DIGNITY. BUT GEORGE BUSH CHANGED THINGS FOREVER WHEN HE ORDERED UP A WAR-HERO VIDEO DURING THE 1988 CAMPAIGN.

TODAY A WAR WOUND GIVES YOU A CRITICAL EDGE. FAR FROM BEING A BAD MEMORY FROM THE DISTANT PAST, A WORLD WAR II INJURY IS A CHERISHED PERSONAL SYMBOL, A BADGE OF HONOR AND SACRIFICE.

DOES MY WOUND STAND IN VIVID CONTRAST TO THE SMOOTH, UNTOUCHED SKIN OF A BILL CLINTON OR PHIL GRAMM, SAY? YOU BE THE JUDGE. LADIES AND GENTLEMEN, PLEASE GIVE A WARM WELCOME TO...

... MY OLD WAR WOUND!

THANK YOU, BOB. THANK YOU. I'M PROUD TO BE A POLITICAL ASSET.

38

39

40

42

44

46

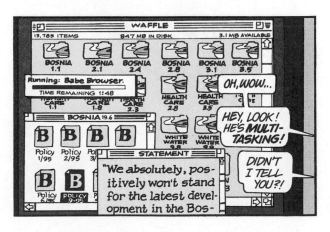

47

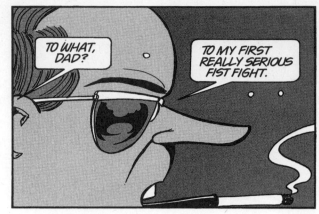

48

49

OH, NO, IT'S ALREADY FRIDAY AND WE STILL HAVE 12 WITNESSES LEFT!

HMM... I'LL SEE WHAT I CAN DO TO FIT 'EM IN...

HE GRABBED ME BY THE SHOULDERS AND KISSED ME ON THE... AND THEN FORCED HIS TONGUE...

PUSHED ME ON COUCH INTO TONGUE MOUTH!

ASKED ME TO MAKE LOVE IN THE...

THEN HE PINNED ME AGAINST THE WALL AND FONDLED ME WITH...

THEN HE RUBBED WITH LEG FORCED TONGUE MOUTH!

FORCIBLY PULLED MY... IN LEG TO SKIRT!

HAVE YOU CONSIDERED BOOKING A SUNDAY?

NO. THESE WOMEN HAVE FAMILIES.

WELL, THAT BRINGS US TO THE END OF OUR TESTIMONY. THERE WILL BE NO ALAN SIMPSON-STYLE GRILLING OF THE VICTIMS ABOUT THEIR PRIVATE LIVES.

AS THE LAW NOW RECOGNIZES, ASKING A SEXUAL ABUSE VICTIM ABOUT HER PAST BEHAVIOR IS AS RELEVANT AS ASKING A ROBBERY VICTIM IF HE'S A SPENDTHRIFT. THE ISSUE IS **CONSENT!**

BEFORE WE LEAVE, WE'D LIKE TO THANK OUR HOSTS FOR MAKING THIS VENUE AVAILABLE TO US. THEY WERE MOST GENEROUS.

HEY, IT WAS OUR PLEASURE!

I DUNNO, I COULD'VE DONE WITHOUT THE TONGUE STUFF.

50

J.J.!

HEY, STRANGER!

WE WERE IN THE NEIGHBORHOOD AND THOUGHT WE'D DROP BY! IF YOU'RE NOT TOO BUSY, I'D LOVE TO HANG AND PICK YOUR BRAIN...

I'M THINKING SERIOUSLY OF GETTING INTO THE MOVIE BUSINESS! I THOUGHT MAYBE YOU COULD GIVE ME AN INSIDER'S TAKE!

BACK UP. WHAT'S THE DEAL WITH THE ADULTERY?

OH, MIKE! IS **THAT** WHAT HE'S CALLING IT?

J.J., I DON'T KNOW **WHAT** YOU THINK YOU'RE DOING!

I CAN'T **BELIEVE** YOU WOULD RUN OUT ON POOR, SWEET, ADORABLE MIKE JUST TO BE WITH SOME... SOME...

IS THAT HIM OVER THERE?

UH-HUH.

ACTUALLY, HE **IS** PRETTY HOT.

THANKS. I GET A LOT OF THAT.

I HOPE YOU GUYS DON'T MIND OUR DROPPING IN LIKE THIS. I KNOW WE SHOULD HAVE CALLED AHEAD...

UM...B.D.? GUESS WHO'S HERE! J.J. AND HER FRIEND ZEKE!

YEAH, RIGHT. LIKE THAT EVIL LITTLE BIMBO AND HER SLEAZE-BAG BOYFRIEND WOULD DARE SHOW THEIR FACES AROUND ANY OF MIKE'S FRIENDS!

HE CAN'T BELIEVE YOU'RE HERE.

ME, NEITHER. BUT I COULD GET USED TO THIS, MAN.

BOOPSIE, IT'S HARD TO EXPLAIN. I JUST COULDN'T TAKE ANOTHER DAY OF SITTING IN THAT GRIMY LOFT WATCHING MIKE SLUMP EVER DEEPER INTO HIS BLACK HOLE!

TOO BAD. BECAUSE TODAY HE'S LIVING THE SWEET LIFE IN SEATTLE, HEAD OF MARKETING FOR A SOFTWARE COMPANY AND HAULING DOWN A HUGE SALARY!

OH.

WELL, LA-DEE-DAH!

LIKE WHAT, SIX FIGURES?

51

ZEKE, HAVE YOU GUYS REALLY THOUGHT THROUGH THE CONSEQUENCES OF YOUR ACTIONS?

OF COURSE WE HAVE, MAN.

BUT IT'S NOT LIKE IT'S THE END OF THE WORLD IF IT DOESN'T WORK OUT. HELL, IF J.J. AND I DON'T MAKE IT, MAYBE I'LL COME BACK AND LOOK YOU UP, OKAY?

UM...THANKS FOR THE LOVELY OFFER, ZEKE, BUT I'M MARRIED.

SO WHAT? SO WAS J.J.!

THIS IS A REPULSIVE HUMAN BEING.

I KNEW YOU'D GET JEALOUS! MAYBE WE SHOULD JUST GO.

BOOPSIE HAS SOME NERVE, DISSING THE MAN I LOVE!

I KNEW THAT CHICK WAS BAD NEWS THE MOMENT I LAID EYES ON HER...

SOME WOMEN THINK THAT JUST BECAUSE THEY'RE BABES, THAT MAKES THEM SPECIAL, KNOW WHAT I MEAN?

YOU HIT ON HER, DIDN'T YOU?

WELL, JUST TO BE POLITE. THERE WAS A VIBE, MAN.

52

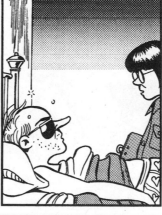

OKAY, BUD—WHAT'S SO IMPORTANT I HAD TO INTERRUPT OUR DAILY PRAYER BREAKFAST?

MR. DUKE? I'M KEVIN DEVILLE FROM CHILD WELFARE SERVICES.

YEAH? SO? WHAT'S THE PROBLEM?

WE RECEIVED AN ANONYMOUS CALL ALERTING US TO NUMEROUS CODE VIOLATIONS OUT HERE.

WHAT? THAT'S IMPOSSIBLE! WE DON'T LET THE KIDS USE THE PHONE...

SHE HAD A CHINESE ACCENT.

YOU DON'T SAY.

MANDARIN OR CANTONESE?

OKAY, LET'S SEE THE SLEEPING QUARTERS...

STRAIGHT AHEAD.

HOW MANY KIDS ARE IN THIS ROOM?

I DUNNO... 35?

35 KIDS IN ONE ROOM?

IT'S PLENTY BIG ENOUGH, SIR. IN CHINA, WE HOUSE TWICE THIS MANY CHILDREN IN A ROOM THIS SIZE.

IN CHINA, YOU KILL THE GIRLS.

YOU PUT TO BOYS TOGETHER?

I WITHDRAW THE COMMENT.

HOW MANY STEPS YOU MISSING THERE? THREE? FOUR?

YOU NEED ME TO DO THE MATH FOR YOU?

MR. DUKE, I'VE NEVER SEEN A CHILD CARE FACILITY IN SUCH POOR CONDITION!

NO KIDDING? NEVER?

Nothin' But Orphans

AND YOU'RE LOW ON EVERYTHING— DISINFECTANTS, SOAP, BAND-AIDS...

BUDGET CUTS! WHAT CAN I DO?

PLENTY OF DUCT TAPE, THOUGH, I SEE...

A NANNY'S BEST FRIEND! NOTICE HOW QUIET IT IS?

ACME

WELL, YOUR BOOKKEEPING IS AS BAD AS EVERYTHING ELSE HERE. WHAT'S THIS BIG CASH DISBURSEMENTS ACCOUNT FOR?

TO MAKE NEW FRIENDS, LIKE YOURSELF, FOR INSTANCE. WE'D LIKE YOU TO BE OUR FRIEND.

OH, REALLY?

REALLY! TAKE WHATEVER YOU NEED. A GUY ON A GOVERNMENT SALARY COULD PROBABLY USE A FEW EXTRA... EXTRA... UM... WHAT ARE YOU DOING?

I'M ABOUT TO HAVE A REALLY BAD DAY, AREN'T I?

YEAH.

SHERIFF'S OFFICE.

YOU TRIED TO **BRIBE** THE INSPECTOR? WHAT WERE YOU THINK-ING, SIR?

I WAS THINKING IT USUAL-LY WORKS. NOW I GOTTA DEAL WITH THE DAMN SHER-IFF...

I'M TOO **OLD** FOR THIS! 20 YEARS AGO, I WOULD'VE JUST GRABBED MY PASSPORT AND KRUGERRANDS, BLOWN UP THE HOUSE, AND ESCAPED IN A HAIL OF GUNFIRE...

BUT NOW... NOW... ≋SIGH≋...

NOW WHAT, SIR?

NOW I JUST WANT TO TAKE A NAP.

WANT ME TO BLOW UP THE HOUSE FOR YOU, DAD?

WHAT'S UP, EARL? WHY THE EMERGENCY MEETING?

BIG TROUBLE, EVERYONE! THE SHERIFF'S COMING OUT AFTER DUKE!

WE CAN'T LET THIS HAPPEN! DUKE MEANS **EVERYTHING** TO US, AND WE HAVE TO MAKE IT CLEAR TO THE SHERIFF THAT IF HE WANTS TO TAKE DUKE, HE'S GONNA HAVE TO GET PAST **US** FIRST! ANY QUESTIONS?

WHO'S DUKE?

THE DRUNK GUY OUT BACK.

WHAT DO YOU SAY— ARE YOU **WITH** ME?

55

DAD? I'VE SPOKEN TO THE OTHER KIDS AND WE'RE ALL BEHIND YOU!

WE'RE NOT GOING TO LET THE SHERIFF TAKE YOU, DAD! NO **WAY!** I GOT EVERYONE PUMPED, TOTALLY FIRED!

SIR? THE SHERIFF JUST PULLED UP...

GOOD GOD, **ALREADY?** WHERE ARE THE KIDS?

NOT TO WORRY. THEY ESCAPED OUT THE BACK.

PROBA-BLY TO FLANK HIM.

GOOD WORK, EARL.

IT'S ALL **BO-GUS,** SHERIFF! SOME BONE-HEAD BUREAU-CRAT WHO...

LOOK, DUKE, YOU KNOW ME — NORMAL-LY I DON'T GIVE A FLY-ING FIG...

BUT YOU GOT **KIDS** OUT HERE! AND THIS GUY'S LISTING 143 SERIOUS CODE VIOLATIONS!

HEY, THE KIDS DON'T CARE! ASK 'EM!

WELL, THAT'S NOT THE WORST OF IT. HE ALSO SAYS YOU TRIED TO BRIBE HIM.

HE DID?

YEAH. SO WHAT GIVES? YOU'VE NEVER OFFERED **ME** A BRIBE!

SHERIFF, YOU'RE LIKE FAMILY! IT NEVER SEEMED NECESSARY!

OKAY, MAYBE I DID TRY TO GREASE THE WHEELS A LITTLE—WAS THAT SO WRONG?

THE FACT IS, I WAS DESPERATE! I'D DO **ANYTHING** FOR THESE KIDS, INCLUDING GOING TO JAIL! THESE ARE **MY** KIDS—ALMOST LIKE A JERRY LEWIS THING—THAT INTENSE.

UH-HUH. WELL, LOOK, DUKE, I'M TOO BUSY TO BOOK YOU RIGHT NOW, SO WHY DON'T YOU JUST VANISH BEFORE I GET BACK, OKAY?

VANISH?

THREE-DAY HEAD START SEEM FAIR?

SIX. I GOTTA DUMP THE KIDS.

HOW LONG WILL YOU BE GONE, DAD?

THERE'S NO TELLING. I'LL BE A FUGITIVE FROM JUSTICE.

CAN'T I COME WITH YOU? WE COULD BE OUTLAWS TOGETHER!

HOW YOU FIGURE? **I'M** THE ONLY ONE IN TROUBLE!

RIGHT, BUT I'D BE **HELPING** YOU! THAT WOULD MAKE ME AN ACCESSORY!

WELL, I GUESS THAT'S RIGHT.

AHEM. WHAT ABOUT HIS EDUCATION?

HEY... WHO ASKED **YOU**?

I'LL JUST PICK HIM UP SOME CD-ROMS OR SOMETHING.

ANYWAY, AFTER WE GET BACK TO ASPEN, I'M **DEFINITELY** GOING TO GET A SHOW OF NEW STUFF OFF THE GROUND...

I MIGHT THEN PARLAY THE RECOGNITION FROM THAT INTO A BOOK OR A MOVIE OR SOMETHING. OR I MIGHT START A MAGAZINE, Y'KNOW?

ZEKE, YOU'VE BEEN AWFULLY QUIET THE LAST FEW MILES. IS SOMETHING WRONG?

NO...WELL, IT'S JUST TOUGH LIVING IN YOUR SHADOW, MAN.

REALLY? SEE, NOW, MIKE WOULD **NEVER** ADMIT THAT.

WHOA...WHAT'S **THIS** GUY'S STORY?

THE JERK'S DRIVING ON THE WRONG SIDE...

OH, MY GOD... LOOK OUT! LOOK OUT!

BEEP!
BEEP!

AIEEE!

WOW... THINK THEY'RE ALL RIGHT?

WHO?

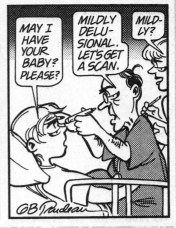

J.J.?

J.J.? IT'S ME, BABE — MIKE...

MIKE, YOUR HUSBAND OF 13 YEARS, NOT SOME SLEAZEBUCKET WHO PICKED YOU UP AND TRASHED YOUR LIFE...

BACK OFF, MAN. YOU'RE CONFUSING HER.

AM I, J.J.? JUST BREATHE IF THE ANSWER'S NO.

SHE'S BEEN LIKE THIS FOR TWO DAYS, MAN. I HAVEN'T LEFT HER SIDE...

WELL, ONCE FOR A MOVIE. AND ONCE TO GET BEER. BUT OTHER THAN THAT, I'VE BEEN HERE FOR HER.

EXCUSE ME, BUT VISITING HOURS ARE OVER, MR. DOONESBURY.

THANKS, MAN.

MR. WHO?

YOU CAN HAVE IT BACK, MAN. IT'S A DORKY NAME ANYWAY.

J.J., WHY DID IT COME TO THIS? WHY DID ANY OF THIS HAVE TO HAPPEN?

WE LOVED EACH OTHER. WE BUILT A LIFE TOGETHER. WE MADE A FAMILY. WHY DID YOU RUN AWAY FROM ALL THAT? I DON'T UNDERSTAND...

IRONIC, ISN'T IT, MAN?

WHAT IS, ZEKE?

SHE WAS NEVER MUCH OF A LISTENER BEFORE.

ZEKE, GO HIT ON A NURSE OR SOMETHING, WOULD YOU?

SO WHAT DO YOU THINK, DOCTOR? IS SHE GOING TO COME OUT OF IT?

QUITE HONESTLY, I CAN'T REALLY SAY. THIS ONE'S GOT ME BAFFLED. AS I TOLD MR. DOONESBURY...

ACTUALLY, I'M MR. DOONESBURY.

YOU ARE?

YES.

SO WHO'S THE GUY ON THE BEER RUN?

I THOUGHT HE WAS A FRIEND OF YOURS. SHOULD WE CALL SECURITY?

60

62

MIKE, I'M SORRY I HURT YOU. IT WASN'T SUPPOSED TO TURN OUT THAT WAY...

I THOUGHT I WAS MAKING SOMETHING *TRUTHFUL*— A PIECE ABOUT PEOPLE CAUGHT IN THE ACT OF EXPRESSING THEIR REAL *FEELINGS*!

I KNOW WHAT YOU'RE THINKING—THAT I WAS BEING SELF-INVOLVED AND GRANDIOSE, THAT ALL I CARED ABOUT WERE MY OWN NEEDS. BUT I DON'T AGREE.

I WAS JUST BEING ME, THE WAY I AM.

DOING WHAT MAKES ME UNIQUE, SPECIAL.

I'M SO GLAD YOU'RE HOME, DAD-O-RAMA!

ME TOO, BABE, YOU GIVE UNCLE BERNIE ANY TROUBLE?

I WAS GOOD AS GOLD. HOW'S MOM?

SHE'S FINE. IT WASN'T SERIOUS. WE'LL SEND HER A CARD TOMORROW.

SHE WAS FAKING IT, WASN'T SHE?

YOUR MOTHER'S AN ARTIST, SWEETHEART. SHE GETS CONFUSED.

WELCOME BACK TO "ALL THINGS RECONSIDERED"! AS ALWAYS, I'M MARK SLACKMEYER, YOUR HOST...

TODAY I'VE GOT A SURPRISE FOR YOU. EVER SINCE I OUTED MYSELF ON THE AIR TWO YEARS AGO, CALLERS HAVE BEEN ASKING ME WHEN I WAS GOING TO FIND SOMEONE TO SHARE MY NEW LIFE WITH.

WELL, IT FINALLY HAPPENED. HIS NAME IS NEIL, AND HE'S WITH US IN THE STUDIO TODAY. WELCOME, NEIL!

THANKS, MARK! HAPPY TO BE HERE!

SO TELL US ABOUT YOURSELF, GUY...

BY POPULAR DEMAND, WE'RE CHATTING TODAY WITH NEIL, MY SIGNIFICANT OTHER. WELCOME, NEIL.

THANKS, MARK!

NEIL, A LOT OF MY LISTENERS WERE BEGINNING TO WONDER IF I'D *EVER* GET INVOLVED WITH SOMEONE. TELL THEM A LITTLE ABOUT YOURSELF.

HAPPY TO, MARK. I'M A FORMER RHODES SCHOLAR, DOCTOR, LECTURER, AUTHOR, JOURNALIST, FILM MAKER AND ARTIST. IN MY SPARE TIME, I BUILD LOW-INCOME HOUSING AND WORK AN AIDS HOT-LINE.

HOW ABOUT *THAT*, GANG? DIDN'T I TELL YOU HE WAS A FIND?

ME? HEY, C'MON, MARK— *YOU'RE* THE CATCH!

65

67

70

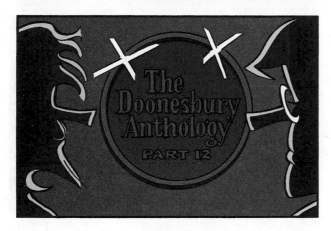

72

73

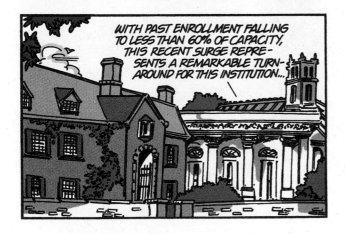

74

76

HMM... WONDER IF IT'S TOO HARD-HITTING...

WHAT DO YOU THINK, NEIL?

IT'S FINE.

...AND CLINTON'S FAILURE TO VETO THE ANTI-GAY MARRIAGE BILL WAS A NEW LOW IN ELECTION-YEAR GUTLESSNESS!

WHAT WERE CLINTON AND CONGRESS THINKING? THAT THEIR OFFICIAL CENSURE WOULD CAUSE GAYS TO RETHINK THEIR SEXUAL ORIENTATION?

DOES THE FAMILY-VALUES CROWD BELIEVE IN THE VALUE OF COMMITMENT OR DON'T THEY?

HERE'S THE IRONY, GANG — COME THE ELECTION, CONSERVATIVES SHOULD BE PREPARED TO ACCEPT FULL CREDIT FOR PROMOTING UNSTABLE, IRRESPONSIBLE GAY RELATIONSHIPS!

THIS HAS BEEN COMMENTARY. I'M MARK SLACKMEYER.

STRONG WORDS FROM A GUY WHO ONLY DATES HIMSELF.

I RESENT THAT, DON'T YOU, NEIL?

SURE DO!

78

80

HEY, DAD— *LOOK!* SHOW-GIRLS!

WHAT *HAPPENED* TO THIS TOWN, TONY? I BARE-LY RECOGNIZE IT ANYMORE!

A LOT OF NEW PLAYERS, DUKE. AND THEY DO THINGS DIFFERENTLY THAN THE OLD OUT-FIT...

WE GOT NEW MANAGEMENT HERE, AND THEY RUN THE JOINT MUCH MORE LIKE A BUSINESS. THESE GUYS ARE REALLY COLD— *TOTALLY* RUTHLESS!

NOT THE *PHILLY* MOB?

NO, NO, TIME-WARNER.

EARL, LET ME ASK YOU SOMETHING. WHEN YOU THINK OF LAS VEGAS, WHAT COMES TO MIND?

LOTS OF COOL STUFF—LIKE THE PYRAMID RIDES, THE EXPLODING VOLCANO, THE AS1 SIM THEATER, WET 'N WILD, GRAND SCAM, YOU NAME IT!

ANY-THING ELSE?

UM... LIKE WHAT?

LIKE *WHAT*? EVER HEARD OF GAMBLING? PROSTITUTION? HELLO?

OH, YOU MEAN THE *PARENT* STUFF! SURE, DAD!

DAMN, I HATE CHANGE...

SON, VOLCANO ERUPTIONS AND TALKING CAESAR STATUES ARE ALL VERY FINE, BUT *THIS* IS WHERE THE REAL MAGIC HAPPENS—THE *CA-SINO!*

THERE ARE OVER 100 MILLION GAMBLERS IN THIS COUNTRY, INCLUDING 4 MILLION PROB-LEM GAMBLERS, 40,000 HIGH ROLLERS, AND COUNTLESS PROFESSIONAL CHEATS...

THE CASINOS IN THIS TOWN CLEAR *SIX BILLION* DOLLARS A YEAR! THAT'S $200 PRO-FIT A SECOND! *MORE* THAN ENOUGH FOR EVERYONE!

INCLUD-ING THE CHEATERS?

I'M GET-TING TO THAT...

REMEMBER, EARL, ON SLOTS, THE HIGHER THE BET, THE LOOSER THE MACHINE. HOUSE TAKE IS ONLY 5% ON DOLLAR SLOTS.

BUT CRAPS ARE BETTER—THE VIG IS ONLY .6%! WITH ROULETTE, YOU GOT A HOUSE ADVANTAGE OF 5.26%.

SO STAY AWAY FROM WHEELS—THEY'RE ALL SUCKER GAMES.

WOW, DAD...

WOW WHAT, KID?

I DUNNO. SOMETIMES YOU SEEM TEN FEET TALL TO ME...

WELL, I'M IN MY ELE-MENT HERE.

82

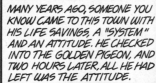

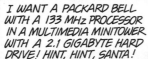

84

88

QUESTION FROM THE FLOOR?

YES, I'M A BUSINESSMAN...

20 YEARS AGO, THE FOLKS AT E.P.A. SHOWED ME THAT BY MANAGING RESOURCES WISELY, OUR COMPANY COULD IN FACT FLOURISH, DOING WELL AND GOOD AT THE SAME TIME...

IT TOOK US A WHILE TO GET IT RIGHT, BUT TODAY WE TAKE PRIDE IN BEING GOOD CORPORATE CITIZENS. WHY ARE YOU TRYING TO ROLL BACK EVERYTHING POSITIVE THAT BUSINESS AND GOVERNMENT HAVE ACCOMPLISHED IN PARTNERSHIP?

I TAKE IT YOU'RE FROM BEN AND JERRY'S...

NO, A POWER COMPANY. COULD YOU ANSWER THE QUESTION?

GOOD MORNING. I'D LIKE TO WELCOME EVERYONE TO THE CYBERCITIZENS-FOR-STEVE-FORBES ORGANIZATIONAL MEETING!

AS YOU KNOW, AT THE CORE OF EVERY GREAT CAMPAIGN ARE THE VOLUNTEERS WHO BELIEVE, WHO SHARE THE DREAM!

I SHARE THE FORBES DREAM OF A FLAT TAX! I BELIEVE! WHO ELSE HERE SHARES THE DREAM? WHO BELIEVES?

YEAH... OVER HERE.

I MIGHT BE GETTING TOO OLD FOR THIS...

CYBERCITIZENS-FOR-STEVE-FORBES HAVE GATHERED AT BERNIE'S BYTE SHACK.

LET'S BE CLEAR WHAT'S AT STAKE, MY FRIENDS...

MOST OF US HERE ARE LOADED UP WITH STOCK OPTIONS! AND WE DESERVE 'EM — WE BUILT THIS INDUSTRY, BUT WHAT'S THE POINT IF WE LOSE IT ALL IN TAXES?

THAT'S WHY THE FORBES CAMPAIGN IS A HOLY CRUSADE! THAT'S WHY WE MUST FIGHT WITH EVERY FIBER IN OUR...

BOB?

WHAT?

COULD WE TAKE A BREAK? I WANT TO CHECK MY E-MAIL.

STEVE FORBES IDENT IN '96

HEY... WHAT'S GOING ON IN HERE?

UM... IT'S A MEETING FOR STEVE FORBES VOLUNTEERS.

OH, YEAH? NOT MUCH OF A TURNOUT.

I KNOW. I ALWAYS SEEM TO BE ATTRACTED TO LOST CAUSES.

WELL, WHAT'S THE POINT OF GETTING INVOLVED IN A CAMPAIGN ANYWAY, YOU KNOW?

TO MEET GIRLS.

TO GIVE SOMETHING BACK.

AS IF! I HAVEN'T GOTTEN ANYTHING YET!

MIND IF I SWING BY MY HOUSE, MIKE? I GOTTA FEED MY CAT...

FINE.

YOU CAN MEET MY HOUSEMATES. MOST OF 'EM ARE STILL UP AT THIS HOUR.

HOUSEMATES? YOU MEAN, OTHER PEOPLE IN THEIR 20s?

UH-HUH. IS THIS A PROBLEM?

THEY'LL ALL BE SPEAKING IN GENERATIONAL CODE. I'LL APPEAR CLUELESS.

GOOD POINT. BETTER WAIT IN THE CAR.

SO WHERE DO YOU WANT TO GO, KIM?

HOW ABOUT CAFÉ CAMEO?

CAFÉ CAMEO?

IT'S A NEW THEME CLUB DEVOTED TO THE NEAR-FAMOUS...

OLD SITCOM STARS, ONE-HIT ROCKERS, ANYONE WHO WAS ALMOST SOMEONE! SOME NIGHTS THE PLACE IS SWARMING WITH PEOPLE WHO LOOK VAGUELY FAMILIAR!

WHAT A DRAW.

YOU NEVER KNOW, MIKE— YOU MIGHT SPOT STEVE FORBES.

92

HI, FOLKS—WELCOME TO CAFÉ CAMEO, HOME OF THE NEAR-GREATS! MY NAME'S CHUCK, AND I'M WORKING THE DOOR TONIGHT.

LISTEN, WOULD YOU GUYS MIND WAITING HERE IN LINE FOR AWHILE? WE'RE TRYING TO MAKE THE CLUB LOOK HOT.

SURE, CHUCK!

OKAY, YOU CAN GO IN. THANKS.

NO PROBLEM.

HEY, LOOK! IT'S WHAT'S-HIS-FACE!

Also Starring

CAFÉ CAMEO. GOTTA LOVE THE THEME.

I KNOW. IT'S SO DOPE...

THE BUZZ ON THIS PLACE IS THAT TWO OF THE ORIGINAL BRADY BUNCH HANG HERE! AND THE SHIRTLESS GUY IN THE COKE COMMERCIAL...

IF I SAW... HEY! OVER THERE, MIKE—LOOK! IT'S WHAT'S-HER-NAME! THE GIRL WHO USED TO PLAY ALL THOSE BIMBOS!

BOOPSIE!

OH...RIGHT, RIGHT! VERY GOOD, MIKE!

I KNOW YOU DON'T QUITE GET THE STEVE FORBES THING, KIM, BUT TRUST ME—HE'S ONE OF US. HE'S A CORE LIBERTARIAN / GEEK!

HE UNDERSTANDS OUR WORLD! HE KNOWS HOW TAXES KILL INCENTIVE! WITH FORBES AS PRESIDENT, WE'LL GET TO KEEP EVERYTHING WHEN WE CASH OUT OF THE STOCK-OPTION LOOP!

LISTEN TO ME.

YOU SAY YOU USED TO LIVE IN A COMMUNE?

SO WHAT ARE YOU DOING HERE ANYWAY, KIM? I THOUGHT YOU WERE IN A SERIOUS CRUNCH MODE TODAY.

WELL, I AM...

BUT I WAS SITTING THERE HUNCHED OVER MY MAC, TOTALLY GEEKED OUT ON A KILLER RUN OF CODE, WHEN SUDDENLY I FELT A MAJOR NEED FOR FACE-TIME WITH MY PERSON!

I'M YOUR PERSON?

IF THAT'S COOL WITH YOU.

UM...SURE! DOES THIS MEAN DATES?

NO, SLEEPOVERS. MIKE, THE DATING THING IS VERY 20 YEARS AGO!

94

LOOK, KIM, BEFORE WE GO ANY FURTHER, I GOTTA ASK YOU— YOU'RE NOT UNCOMFORTABLE WITH OUR AGE DIFFERENCE?

NOT AT ALL. WHY WOULD I BE?

MIKE, I GREW UP IN A WORLD DOMINATED BY BOOMERS. YOUR CULTURE WAS INESCAPABLE. AND LETTERMAN GAVE MY AGE GROUP THE TOOLS TO ASSIMILATE.

IT'S TRUE I DIDN'T EXPERIENCE THE NUCLEAR FAMILY, DISCO AND '60s T.V. FIRST-HAND, BUT BY THE TIME I WAS 15, I COULD REFER TO ALL OF THEM IN A HIP, KNOWING WAY.

AMAZING... I DIDN'T GO IRONIC UNTIL I WAS 30!

QUIZ ME ON "GILLIGAN'S ISLAND." GO AHEAD, ASK ME ANYTHING!

SEE, MIKE, EVEN WITH THE AGE DISPARITY, WE'RE NOT THAT DIFFERENT. SURE, YOU CAME BY YOUR CYNICISM THROUGH YEARS OF DISILLUSIONMENT, WHEREAS I SIMPLY GREW UP CYNICAL...

BUT ON PLANET DOWNSIZE, RANDOM DESPAIR BECOMES THE DEFAULT PARADIGM FOR ALL WORKER BEES! IT'S WHERE THE GENERATIONS—YOUR TRIBE AND MINE—NOW CONVERGE!

WANT ME TO SCROLL THAT BY YOU AGAIN?

PLEASE. AND COULD I HAVE A HARD COPY?

YOU KNOW, KIM, I'M NOT SO SURE THE SLEEPOVER PART OF OUR RELATIONSHIP IS GOING TO WORK OUT...

WHAT? WHY NOT?

WELL, YOU LIVE IN A GROUP HOUSE WITH FIVE OTHER TECHIES, AND I LIVE IN A CONDO WITH A SEVEN-YEAR-OLD. NEITHER PLACE IS VERY CONDUCIVE TO A COURTSHIP.

"COURTSHIP"? DID YOU REALLY JUST SAY "COURTSHIP", MIKE?

I DID, BUT TO MY CREDIT, I INSTANTLY REGRETTED IT.

YOU'RE SECOND-GENERATION GEEK, AREN'T YOU?

ALEX, I'D LIKE YOU TO MEET DADDY'S NEW FRIEND, KIM ROSENTHAL...

HI, ALEX!

LISTEN, I HAVE TO MAKE A FEW CALLS, SO WHY DON'T YOU GUYS JUST HANG FOR AWHILE, OKAY?

I ALREADY HAVE A MOTHER.

SO DO I. WANT TO PLAY THE NEW NBA ALL-STARS?

YOU'VE GOT THE NEW NBA ALL-STARS DISK?

EVEN BETTER—I'VE GOT THE 1997 BETA VERSION!

GET OUT! WHO GAVE IT TO YOU?

WE'RE PUBLISHING IT. I'M DOING THE BUG-CHECKING.

YOU'RE A BUG-CHECKER? THAT'S YOUR JOB?

SOMETIMES. WHY?

WHY? BUG-CHECKING IS BRUTALLY COOL!

AH, ANOTHER CRAZY KID WITH A DREAM.

SO CHECK THIS OUT, OKAY? IF YOU CLICK ON DENNIS RODMAN'S SNEAKERS, HIS HAIR CHANGES COLOR!

THAT'S SO AWESOME!

IT'S WHAT WE CALL EASTER EGG FUNCTIONALITY—A LITTLE SURPRISE FOR THOSE IN THE KNOW...

YOU KNOW, KIM, I'M SO GLAD IT'S YOU WHO'S DADDY'S FRIEND! WHEN HE TOLD ME HE WAS SEEING SOMEONE AT WORK, I WAS AFRAID THAT... THAT...

THAT WHAT, ALEX?

I WAS AFRAID SHE MIGHT BE FROM MARKETING.

YOU POOR KID! WHY DIDN'T YOU JUST ASK?

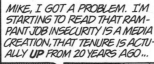

THERE IS ONE GLIMMER OF GOOD NEWS, MIKE — AT LEAST FOR YOU PERSONALLY...

SINCE OUR PROBLEM IS A MARKETING ONE, WE WON'T BE CUTTING ANYONE FROM YOUR DEPARTMENT.

OH, YEAH? THEN WHO *DOES* GET IT?

THE GEEK CORPS. WE'LL HAVE TO SHED AT LEAST 50 CODERS.

CODERS?

HOPE YOU HAVEN'T GOTTEN TOO CLOSE TO ANYONE...

CODERS? DID YOU SAY YOU WERE FIRING CODERS?

YEAH. I'VE GOT THE LIST RIGHT HERE...

MY GOD! **KIM'S** ON HERE! YOU WANT ME TO AX MY OWN GIRLFRIEND!

HMM..., THAT DOES SEEM A LOT TO ASK...

TELL YOU WHAT, MIKE, YOU'RE IN CHARGE. IF YOU CAN'T GET YOURSELF TO FIRE KIM, PICK SOMEONE ELSE TO FIRE. IT'LL BE YOUR CHOICE.

CHOICE? *CHOICE?* YOU CALL THAT A *CHOICE?*

MIKE, I WOULDN'T GIVE IT TO YOU IF I DIDN'T THINK YOU COULD HANDLE IT.

WELL, MIKE, I'M OFF TO MAUI. SORRY TO LEAVE YOU WITH SUCH A TROUBLED BROW...

IF YOU NEED ANY MORAL SUPPORT, YOU CAN REACH ME AT THE ROYAL WAIHEE BEACH HOTEL, OKAY?

UH... MIKE?

CAN I FIRE THEM BY E-MAIL?

OF COURSE NOT. IF WE WERE THAT KIND OF COMPANY, **I'D** DO IT!

WE'RE BACK, AND THE TOPIC IS STILL DOWNSIZING! IS THE CALLER ON THE LINE?

YEAH, MARK, I HAVE A FRIEND WHO'S BEEN TOLD BY HIS BOSS TO EITHER FIRE HIS GIRLFRIEND OR CHOOSE SOMEONE ELSE TO FIRE IN HER PLACE...

WHAT DO YOU THINK MY FRIEND SHOULD DO?

HARD TO SAY. EITHER WAY, THE GUY'S SCUM.

THAT'S WHAT I THOUGHT...

WHO YOU FIRING, DAD?

98

WHAT ARE YOU SAYING, MAN? AM I BEING FIRED?

UM... WELL, YEAH, SORT OF.

SEE, A BIG ACCOUNT BLEW UP ON US, SO WE HAVE TO DOWNSIZE THE CODING DEPARTMENT...

IT'S NOTHING PERSONAL, KIM. BERNIE'S HAPPY WITH YOUR WORK. BUT WE HAD TO LOSE 50 CODERS, AND YOUR NAME UNFORTUNATELY MADE THE LIST.

BUT MY NAME ISN'T KIM.

KID! KID! I MEANT KID!

FINISHED FIRING ALL MY FRIENDS?

KIM...

WERE YOU SAVING ME FOR LAST, OR DID SOMEONE ELSE GET AXED IN MY PLACE?

KIM, LISTEN...

I'M ALL EARS.

WHAT WAS I SUPPOSED TO DO? I WAS GIVEN A TERRIBLE CHOICE—LOSE YOU OR LOSE MY SELF-RESPECT! I CHOSE YOU!

WRONG CHOICE, I QUIT.

AARGH!

QUIT? YOU **CAN'T** QUIT! NOT AFTER WHAT I PUT MYSELF THROUGH!

A FAVOR I DID **NOT** ASK FOR!

I KNOW, BUT WHAT ELSE COULD I DO? I'M A MIDDLE-AGED DIVORCÉ WITH A KID AND A FAIRLY HUGE SELF-ESTEEM DEFICIT. I NEVER EXPECTED SOMEONE LIKE YOU IN MY LIFE.

THE THOUGHT OF LOSING YOU IS UNBEARABLE! NOW THAT I'VE FOUND YOU, I...I...

WHAT'S GOING ON? I DON'T USUALLY SOUND LIKE A SOAP OPERA CHARACTER.

I FIND THAT HARD TO BELIEVE.

OKAY, KIM, MAYBE I **DID** MAKE THE WRONG CHOICE, BUT I MADE IT BECAUSE OF YOU! I DIDN'T WANT TO LOSE YOU...

LOSE ME? WHY WOULD YOU LOSE ME? IT'S JUST A JOB, MIKE. I **EXPECT** TO HAVE LOTS OF JOBS IN MY LIFE. IN FACT, I'VE ALREADY BEEN OFFERED A NEW ONE!

YOU HAVE? WHERE?

A COMPANY IN PARIS. BUT WITH E-MAIL, WE COULD GO VIRTUAL.

VIRTUAL? YOU WANT A **VIRTUAL** RELATIONSHIP?

WELL, SURE, WHY NOT? THE TECHNOLOGY'S ONLY GOING TO GET BETTER.

SO WHAT'S YOUR FRIEND DOING IN VIETNAM?

WELL, HE'S INVOLVED IN SOME SORT OF JOINT VENTURE...

APPARENTLY YOU CAN'T REALLY DO BUSINESS THERE UNLESS YOU HAVE A VIETNAMESE PARTNER...

BASICALLY THE ARRANGEMENT IS **YOU** POUR IN A LOT OF MONEY, AND YOUR PARTNER SECURES ALL THE NECESSARY PERMITS.

PERMITS TO DO WHAT?

TO POUR IN MORE MONEY. IT SORT OF REMINDS ME OF THE WAR...

GEORGE THINKS VIETNAM IS THE NEXT ASIAN ECONOMIC POWERHOUSE, THAT WITH HER RESOURCES, THE SKY'S THE LIMIT!

HE FEELS THAT HE'S GOTTEN IN ON THE GROUND FLOOR, THAT RIGHT NOW IS A TIME OF EXTRAORDINARY INVESTMENT OPPORTUNITY!

YEAH, BUT IS HE ACTUALLY MAKING MONEY?

HE SAYS HE WILL BE. MAYBE. IT'S TOO SOON TO TELL, REALLY.

VIETNAM SOUNDS A LOT LIKE THE WEB.

WELL, HE'S ONLY ON HIS THIRD ROUND OF BRIBES.

102

SO WHAT ELSE DOES GEORGE SAY?

WELL, HE'S INVITING ME TO VISIT HIM IN VIETNAM...

MY GOSH... WOULD YOU EVEN CONSIDER IT?

WELL, I DON'T KNOW. MAYBE IT'S FINALLY TIME. IT MIGHT HELP EXORCISE A FEW DEMONS.

WHAT DO YOU MEAN?

WELL, LIKE MY NIGHTMARES. FOR YEARS, I'VE HAD THIS RECURRING DREAM ABOUT BEING TRAPPED IN A FIREFIGHT.

A FIRE-FIGHT? HERE IN L.A.?

YEAH. SO A CHANGE OF SCENERY MIGHT DO ME GOOD.

MAYBE I **SHOULD** GO BACK TO VIETNAM, BOOPSIE. AS A KIND OF CLOSURE.

BUT DON'T YOU HAVE LOTS OF BAD ASSOCIATIONS WITH VIETNAM?

WELL, SURE, OF COURSE. BUT ON ANOTHER LEVEL, I LOVED IT. IT'S THE DARK SECRET OF LOTS OF SOLDIERS—THEY LOVED COMBAT, ITS INTENSITY...

I DUNNO... IT'S HARD TO EXPLAIN.

YOU DON'T HAVE TO, B.D.—I UNDERSTAND.

NO, YOU DON'T, BOOP-SIE—UNLESS YOU'VE...

B.D., I SERVED IN THE PUNIC WARS. SO DON'T PATRONIZE ME.

ARE YOU SURE YOU FEEL UP TO THIS TRIP, B.D.?

I'M SURE.

BUT YOU'VE BEEN SICK OFF AND ON FOR A YEAR...

I'LL BE FINE, BOOPSIE.

HOW LONG WILL YOU BE GONE?

TWO WEEKS. IT TAKES FOREVER TO GET TO VIETNAM. IT'S ACROSS THE INTERNATIONAL DATELINE.

WELL, CALL ME YESTERDAY.

IT'S NOT YESTERDAY THERE. IT'S TOMORROW. THAT'S HOW THEY ESCAPE THE PAST...

©B Trudeau

EXCUSE ME, YOU'RE NOT BY ANY CHANCE VIETNAMESE, ARE YOU?

YES, I AM.

I'M AMERICAN. I SERVED IN YOUR COUNTRY BACK IN '72!

IS THAT RIGHT?

RELAX, I'M NOT GOING TO BITE. I COME IN PEACE.

THAT'S NICE. NILES? HOW DID HONG KONG OPEN?

©B Trudeau

103

SO TELL ME—DOES IT MAKE YOU UNCOMFORTABLE SITTING NEXT TO ME? YOU KNOW, AN AMERICAN, A FORMER "PIRATE"?

THE WALL STREET JOURNAL

NOT REALLY. THE LIBERATION WAS 20 YEARS AGO. WE'VE HAD TWO MORE WARS SINCE THEN. I WASN'T EVEN BORN WHEN YOU WERE IN VIETNAM.

OH... WELL, YEAH, I CAN SEE HOW IT MIGHT ALL SEEM LIKE ANCIENT HISTORY TO YOU, THEN...

AMAZING! CAN YOU **BELIEVE** HOW THE YEN IS TRADING?

WE COULD HAVE WON, YOU KNOW, IF WE'D REALLY WANTED TO.

THE WALL STREET JOURNAL

©B Trudeau

I DON'T GET IT— YOU DON'T FEEL **ANY** RESENTMENT TOWARD AMERICA?

RESENTMENT? WHAT'S TO RESENT?

AMERICA'S OUR MODEL— OUR PARADIGM OF CHOICE. IN THINKING ABOUT A BETTER LIFE, AMERICA HELPS US IMAGINE WHERE WE'D LIKE TO BE.

INCREDIBLE...

©B Trudeau

SO WE **DID** WIN YOUR HEARTS AND MINDS!

IS **THAT** WHAT YOU WERE GOING FOR? NO ONE COULD TELL.

FRIEND, YOU CAN'T IMAGINE WHAT THAT WAR WAS LIKE. I SPENT SIX MONTHS OF PURE HELL OUT IN THE FIELD.

REALLY? MY FATHER FOUGHT AGAINST BOTH THE FRENCH AND THE AMERICANS. HE LOST NINE MEMBERS OF HIS FAMILY AND 15 YEARS OF HIS LIFE FIGHTING FROM A TUNNEL.

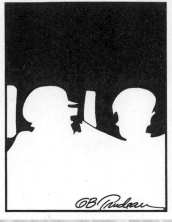

WELL, LA-DEE-DAH.

YOU STARTED IT.

THE WALL STREET JOURNAL

IT WAS GREAT OF YOU TO PICK ME UP, GEORGE. WITH A LIMO, NO LESS!

WELL, YOU CAN THANK MY PARTNER, B.D.! HE'S THE ONE WITH THE PERKS...

WHO'S YOUR PARTNER?

HE'S A WELL-WIRED PARTY TYPE—LIKE ALL THE VIETNAMESE INVOLVED IN FOREIGN INVESTMENT...

WE CALL THEM THE VC² — THE VIET CONG VENTURE CAPITALISTS.

AND THEY'RE GOOD AT THIS?

NOT AT ALL. BUT THEY'RE HUNGRY. LITERALLY.

...AND THERE'S THE REX HOTEL, WHERE THE OFFICERS HUNG OUT! MAN, IT HASN'T CHANGED ONE BIT!

NOPE. IT'S STILL THE COLONIAL HOTEL OF CHOICE...

AND THERE'S THE OPERA HOUSE! AND THE CONTINENTAL...

AND... AND... WOW...

WHAT?

I CAN'T GET OVER ALL THE MARLBORO AND PEPSI SIGNS!

I KNOW. IT TURNS OUT WE WON.

WHAT'S THIS PLACE, GEORGE?

THE Q BAR. IT'S AN EXPAT JOINT. THOUGHT YOU MIGHT LIKE A NIGHTCAP.

YOU THOUGHT RIGHT, BUDDY...

WHY, IT'S MR. TRINH!

B.D., SAY HELLO TO VO THI TRINH, FORMER V.C. COLONEL. HE SERVED BELOW US OUT AT FIREBASE BUNDY!

BELOW US?

YEAH, IN A TUNNEL! RIGHT UNDER THE MESS TENT!

WE USED TO LISTEN TO YOUR MOVIES.

IN MIKE'S SUMMER DAYDREAM, HE'S WOWING WALL STREET.

SO THAT'S THE BERNIE'S BYTE SHACK STORY, LADIES AND GENTLEMEN...

AS WE PROCEED TOWARD OUR INITIAL PUBLIC OFFERING, WE WELCOME YOUR INQUIRIES. THANK YOU FOR COMING—

TREMENDOUS! / BRILLIANT!

MIKE! HOW CAN I GET IN EARLY?

MIKE! A MINUTE!

THE BRIEFING GOES WELL.

I'D BE WILLING TO BREAK THE LAW!

ME TOO!

MIKE, OVER HERE!

IN MIKE'S SUMMER DAYDREAM, HE'S PITCHING THE HIGH-TECH BUSINESS PRESS...

WELL, THAT'S THE DOG-AND-PONY SHOW, FOLKS...

NOW YOU KNOW WHY BERNIE'S BYTE SHACK IS APPROACHING ITS OFFERING WITH A FAIR DEGREE OF CONFIDENCE!

ANY QUES- TIONS?

YES, MR. DOONESBURY, IF WHAT YOU SAY IS TRUE, YOU BOYS COULD VIRTUALLY **RULE** THE INTERNET WITHIN A MATTER OF DAYS! ARE YOU READY?

VERY MUCH SO. NEITHER OF US HAS A LIFE.

WE FEEL THAT LIVES ARE FOR WIMPS.

THE BIG DAY.

SO HOW'RE WE DOING, BERN?

WELL, GREAT, AT FIRST. WE OPENED AT $12.50 A SHARE, AND THE FLOOR WENT NUTS...

BUT THERE'S BEEN NO MOVE- MENT AT **ALL** FOR THE LAST 20 MINUTES!

NONE?

NONE. IT'S STALLED AT $600.

HMM... MAYBE EVERYONE'S RELOADING.

BEEN QUITE A WEEK, HASN'T IT, MIKE?

YOU SAID IT! I'M ONLY SORRY KIM WASN'T HERE TO SHARE IT WITH ME.

BOY, DO I MISS HER! I WISH... WISH ...!

WHAT? WHAT IS IT, MIKE?

I JUST WON A TRIP TO **PARIS**! FROM A BOTTLECAP!

MAN! THIS IS ALL LIKE OUT OF A DREAM, YOU KNOW?

...AND COMING UP ON "GOOD MORNING, HO CHI MINH CITY"...

...GENERAL GIAP'S PERSONAL TRAINER!

...AND WELCOME BACK TO "GOOD MORNING, HO CHI MINH CITY," WHERE WE'RE STILL TALKING TO **JIMMY RAY THUDPUCKER!**

JIMMY, YOU AND YOUR BAND, HEARTS & MINDS, SEEM TO BE ENJOYING QUITE A RUN DOWN AT APOCALYPSE NOW...

YEAH, IT'S TURNED INTO A GREAT GIG. WE'VE ALMOST BECOME THE HOUSE BAND.

VIETNAMESE FANS ARE REAL SUPPORTIVE OF THE '70s COUNTRY-ROCK THING THAT WE DO. OUR SOUND JUST SEEMS TO HAVE TAKEN OFF!

IN FACT, I'M BACK IN THE STUDIO RIGHT NOW RECORDING SOME '70s CLASSICS — INCLUDING A VIETNAMESE OLDIE!

REALLY? WHICH ONE?

"HE WHO COMES TO CU CHI, THE BRONZE FORTRESS IN THE LAND OF IRON, WILL COUNT THE CRIMES ACCUMULATED BY THE ENEMY."

GREAT CHOICE! WILL YOU BE MAKING A VIDEO?

AFRAID NOT. I CAN'T AFFORD ALL THE PERMITS.

116

118

120

HEY, READERS! REMEMBER OUR **1991 ORGANIZATIONAL CHART,** WHICH SORTED OUT OUR CAST OF CHARACTERS FOR CONFUSED READERS? WELL, FIVE YEARS LATER, SOME OF YOU REPORT YOU'RE **STILL** CONFUSED!

AS PROFESSIONAL COMMUNICATORS, WE FEEL BAD ABOUT THAT, SO WE'VE CREATED A GREATLY SIMPLIFIED **CAST PORTRAIT AND KEY!** IDENTIFYING THE CHARACTERS HAS NEVER BEEN EASIER! **ENJOY!**

CAST KEY

Progenitor of BUTTS (26), ex-ad man MIKE (6), son of the WIDOW D. (15) and brother of Dr. Whoopie rep SAL (14), is freshly divorced from artist J.J. (16) (lover of ZEKE (17) and daughter of legal eagle JOANIE (1), who is married to reporter RICK (10)), and has moved with daughter ALEX (7) to Seattle, where he's fallen in love with GenX coder KIM (5) while working for technocrat BERNIE (34), a former roommate (at a college presided over by KING (28) and chaplained by SCOT (18)), as is state trooper B.D. (8) (friend of fellow vet RAY (19) and former adversary of PHRED (25)); his superstarlet wife BOOPSIE (9), who is repped by SID (29) and whose daughter SAM (2) is nannied by retired tannist ZONKER (4) (honorific nephew of DUKE (12), who with son EARL (11) has left love-slave HONEY (13) to settle in Las Vegas); and gay radio jock MARK (3) (son of financier PHIL (30), a friend of oil tycoon JIM (35), who is a colleague of correspondent ROLAND (20), interviewer of homeless couple ALICE (24) and ELMONT (23), and a fan of JIMMY (22), whose benefit record for GINNY (32), wife to cookie czar CLYDE (31), failed to help her defeat LACEY (21) in her bid for Congress now led by NEWT (27) in opposition to BILL (33).

WONDER IF JEFF IS SPEAKING WITH US TODAY...

...OR IF THERE'S BEEN ANOTHER OVERNIGHT HORMONE SURGE.

HEY, RICK, WHATEVER HAPPENED WITH CHELSEA CLINTON'S APPLICATION TO WALDEN?

IT WAS WITHDRAWN. THE KID WHO SENT IT IN APOLOGIZED, AND NONE OF US WROTE ANOTHER WORD ABOUT IT.

YOU KNOW, IT'S KIND OF AMAZING HOW PROTECTIVE THE PRESS HAS BECOME OF HER...

I THINK BECAUSE CHELSEA'S SUCH A NICE, BRIGHT, POLITE, WELL-ADJUSTED TEEN-AGER, WE'VE ALL DECIDED SHE'S A NATIONAL TREASURE.

I MEAN, IT'S SO RARE THAT...

GOT IT, DAD! MESSAGE RECEIVED LOUD AND CLEAR, OKAY?

WAS THAT REALLY NECESSARY, RICK?

WHAT? WHAT JUST HAPPENED?

124

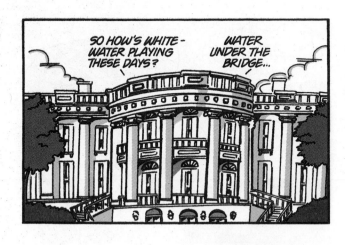

129

...AND WE FEEL CLINTON'S DEFENSE OF THE ANTI-GAY MARRIAGE BILL WAS A TERRIBLE SLAP IN THE FACE!

WELL, THERE YOU HAVE IT, MARK— *ANOTHER* DELEGATE ABANDONED, FORSAKEN BY HIS OWN PARTY!

THIS IS ONE GAY, DEMOCRATIC ACTIVIST WHO'S FEELING *VERY* LONELY JUST NOW, MARK!

UM... IS HE CUTE?

BEATS ME. I DON'T HAVE MY CONTACTS IN.

ELMONT? YOU STILL THERE, BUDDY?

YES, MARK, AND I'M STANDING NEXT TO A NEW YORK DELEGATE, DRESSED CASUALLY IN A PEARL GRAY DONNA KARAN ENSEMBLE!

HELLO, LADY, I'M ELMONT DOE FOR FOX NEWS! WHAT I WANT TO KNOW IS WHY THE PARTY HAS ABANDONED THE PRIDE OF OUR CITY STREETS— THE SANITY-CHALLENGED?

DO YOU KNOW WHAT IT'S *LIKE* TO EXPERIENCE CHRONIC MOOD SWINGS? DO YOU KNOW WHAT IT'S *LIKE* TO HEAR A VOICE IN YOUR HEAD FOR *DAYS* RUNNING?

UH... ELMONT, THAT'S JUST ME.

THERE IT IS *AGAIN!*

SECURITY!

SO WHAT DOES CLINTON'S RIGHTWARD MARCH MEAN? HAS THIS "NEW DEMOCRAT" *REALLY* RENOUNCED EVERYTHING HIS PARTY HAS TRADITIONALLY STOOD FOR?

OR IS THE MOVE ONLY AN ELECTION YEAR FEINT, AFTER WHICH HE'LL RETURN TO HIS OLD PROGRESSIVE AGENDA?

IN ANY CASE, I GUESS THAT ABOUT WRAPS UP OUR CONVENTION COVERAGE, EH, ELMONT?

NOT SO, MARK. I'M STANDING HERE WITH AL GORE...

NEW JERSEY

CAMPBELL, AM I DREAMING? ARE THESE BUDGET NUMBERS REAL?

YES, SIR. WALDEN IS FINALLY BACK IN THE BLACK!

HOW IS THIS POSSIBLE?

TUITION HIKES PLUS GETTING RID OF TENURE.

AMAZING— AND WE CAN STILL ATTRACT COMPETENT FACULTY?

TRUST ME, SIR. IT'S A BUYER'S MARKET.

OKAY, WE NEED TWO ROMANTIC LIT INSTRUCTORS TODAY!

HERE! OVER HERE!

ICI!

134

I CAN'T BELIEVE ANYONE WOULD SHUT DOWN THE CANNABIS BUYERS' CLUB! WHO ORDERED THE BUST?

DAN LUNGREN, THE STATE ATTORNEY GENERAL. THE LOCAL COPS WOULDN'T DO IT, SO THEY HAD TO BRING IN REPUBLICANS.

REPUBLICANS? ARE YOU SURE?

WHO **ELSE** WOULD RAID A SANCTUARY FOR DYING AIDS AND CANCER PATIENTS?

DEMOCRATS. IT'S AN ELECTION YEAR.

WELL, OKAY, BUT THEY WOULDN'T USE A BATTERING RAM!

BUSTING A BUYERS' CLUB! WHAT A WORLD!

WELL, IF PROP 215 IS APPROVED, IT'LL NEVER HAPPEN AGAIN...

WHAT'S PROP 215?

A VOTER REFERENDUM ON MEDICAL MARIJUANA. IT'D ALLOW DOCTORS TO PRESCRIBE POT.

REALLY?

UH-HUH.

OKAY, SAY I HAD HAY FEVER...

YOU'D HAVE TO FIND A **REALLY** BAD DOCTOR WHO THOUGHT IT WAS CANCER.

MAN, IT SOUNDS LIKE PROP 215 COULD CHANGE EVERYTHING FOR US!

YEAH, BUT IT DOESN'T SOLVE OUR IMMEDIATE CRISIS...

I KNOW YOU'RE NOT PART OF THE RETAIL SCENE ANYMORE, BUT CAN YOU THINK OF **ANYONE** WHO COULD GET US AN EMERGENCY SHIPMENT?

WELL, I COULD TRY LUIS. HE'S AN OLD STONER FRIEND OF MINE WHO GOT KICKED OUT OF HIGH SCHOOL...

WHAT'S HE DO?

NO ONE KNOWS. BUT HE **HAS** BECOME A MILLIONAIRE.

YEAH, TRY LUIS.

...ANYWAY, LUIS, OUR FOLKS ARE HURTING, AND IT'D BE GREAT IF YOU COULD DONATE SOME POT TO GET US BY...

YEAH, WELL, I'D LOVE TO HELP, MAN, BUT I'M TAPPED OUT. I'M **ALWAYS** GETTING HIT UP FOR CHARITY GIGS!

YOU ARE?

ALL THE TIME, MAN.

LIKE WHAT?

WELL, LIKE, I HAD TO CATER JERRY GARCIA'S FUNERAL...

...AND FOLLOWING THE BUST, ALL OUR REGULAR SUPPLIERS ARE LAYING LOW!

YOU'VE BEEN SUCH A GOOD FRIEND TO US IN THE PAST, I THOUGHT MAYBE...

LOOK, KID, I JUST DON'T DEAL ANYMORE! ALL I HAVE IS MY PERSONAL STASH!

I KNOW, I KNOW, BUT EVERY LITTLE BIT WILL HELP! YOU SHOULD SEE THESE FOLKS — THEY'RE DYING, SUFFERING TERRIBLY, NAUSEOUS, WASTING AWAY...

OKAY, *OKAY!* I'LL SEND YOU MY LAST TON! BUT THAT'S IT!

OH, GREAT. NOW YOU'LL BE CRABBY ALL WEEKEND.

GOOD EVENING. FOR WEEKS NOW, BOB DOLE HAS BEEN TRYING, UNSUCCESSFULLY, TO ENFLAME VOTERS OVER CLINTON'S 'CHARACTER' PROBLEM...

DOES PUBLIC DISINTEREST MEAN DOLE'S CHARGES ARE WITHOUT MERIT? NOT AT ALL! HERE TO HELP US SORT IT ALL OUT IS G.O.P. THINK-TANKIST CHASE TALBOTT III!

CHASE, WALK US THROUGH THE CASE BOB DOLE HAS FAILED TO MAKE. WHAT *ARE* THE BIG "CHARACTER" ISSUES HERE?

OKAY, FIRST OF ALL, WHITEWATER...

BORING. WHAT ELSE YOU GOT?

G.O.P. ANALYST CHASE TALBOTT III, TAKES ON THE CHARACTER ISSUE.

BASICALLY, WE'RE TALKING ABOUT THE MOST ETHICALLY CHALLENGED WHITE HOUSE IN A CENTURY!

TO DATE, OVER 30 MEMBERS OF THIS ADMINISTRATION HAVE BEEN INVOLVED IN MISDEEDS OR...

OKAY. HOLD IT RIGHT THERE, CHASE...

REAGAN HAD OVER *100* UNDERLINGS IN TROUBLE. AND THEIR WRONGDOING WAS *FAR* MORE SERIOUS! YET THE PUBLIC FORGAVE REAGAN — SHOULDN'T CLINTON GET THE SAME PASS?

NO. CLINTON'S A LIBERAL — HE SHOULD *KNOW* BETTER.

OKAY. JUST CHECKING.

AND THEN THERE'S THE MATTER OF THE ILLEGAL $250,000 THAT HAD TO BE RETURNED TO A SOUTH KOREAN COMPANY...

NOT TO MENTION A *HIGHLY* SUSPECT $452,000 FROM AN INDONESIAN COUPLE!

HMM... VERY INTERESTING, CHASE.

OKAY, EVERYBODY WHO'S SHOCKED THAT A POLITICAL PARTY ACCEPTED SPECIAL INTEREST MONEY, CALL IN NOW!

YOU... YOU PLAY TO THE WORST IN YOUR AUDIENCE, DON'T YOU?

NEW TO TALK RADIO, ARE WE, CHASE?

137

Panel 1: LASTLY, I JUST WANT TO WISH YOU AND CHASE ALL THE BEST...

Panel 2: ...ALTHOUGH, I MUST SAY, I SURE AM GOING TO MISS NEIL.

Panel 3: ME, TOO. THANKS, CALLER. / WHO'S NEIL?

Panel 4: UH... NOBODY. / NOBODY? SO WILL I BE NOBODY ONE DAY?

Panel 1: ANY QUESTIONS? YES, JIM. / YEAH, NEWT, A LOT OF PEOPLE GO TO PARKS TO GET AWAY FROM COMMERCIALIZATION. IS THE PUBLIC GOING TO GO FOR THIS?

Panel 2: ABSOLUTELY! PEOPLE LOVE IT WHEN CORPORATIONS STEP UP TO SUPPORT PUBLIC ATTRACTIONS! JUST LOOK AT THE OLYMPICS!

Panel 3: ?

Panel 4: OKAY, MAYBE THAT'S NOT SUCH A GOOD MODEL... / SHOULD WE STRIKE IT FROM OUR SHEETS, NEWT?

Panel 1: NEWT, IT SEEMS TO ME THAT PARK SPONSORSHIPS COULD BE PRETTY PRICEY FOR PRIVATE INDUSTRY. WHAT'S THE UPSIDE FOR US?

Panel 2: GOOD WILL, PHIL—ESPECIALLY FOR THOSE OF YOU IN THE EXTRACTION INDUSTRIES! IT'S MONEY IN THE BANK FOR A RAINY DAY!

Panel 3: SAY YOU'RE EXXON, AND YOU HAVE A MASSIVE OIL SPILL UP ON THE TUNDRA—WHAT STANDS BETWEEN YOU AND A P.R. NIGHTMARE?

Panel 4: THE EXXON WILDFLOWER PRESERVE? / BINGO! YOU'RE THE GREENEST GUY ON THE BLOCK!

Panel 1: NEWT, I SEE HERE THAT THE INTERIOR SECRETARY WILL ENJOY BROAD AUTHORITY IN GRANTING PARK SPONSORSHIPS. HOW DO WE KNOW BABBITT WON'T STONEWALL US?

Panel 2: GOT IT COVERED. WE SIMPLY KEEP SLASHING AWAY AT INTERIOR'S BUDGET, EVENTUALLY MAKING THE SYSTEM DEPENDENT ON CORPORATE LARGESSE!

Panel 3: PICTURE IT, FOLKS—BRUCE BABBITT, ON HIS HANDS AND KNEES, BEGGING YOU TO PUT UP BILLBOARDS IN OUR NATIONAL PARKS!

Panel 4: NOW THAT'S A KODAK MOMENT! I'M IN! / ME, TOO! / NEWT, COULD WE RENAME YOSEMITE "MARLBORO COUNTRY"?

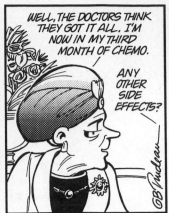

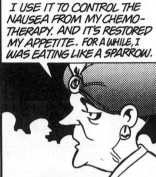

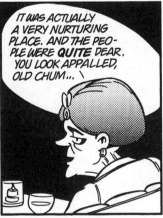

MILLIE, WHY DO YOU HAVE TO USE MARIJUANA? I THOUGHT THERE WAS A SYNTHETIC VERSION...

WELL, THERE IS, BUT IT'S EXPENSIVE, SLOW-WORKING, AND HARD FOR ME TO KEEP DOWN...

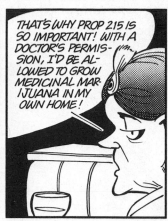

THAT'S WHY PROP 215 IS SO IMPORTANT! WITH A DOCTOR'S PERMISSION, I'D BE ALLOWED TO GROW MEDICINAL MARIJUANA IN MY OWN HOME!

YOUR HOME, MILLIE? ARE YOU SERIOUS?

ABSOLUTELY, DEAR.

BUT... BUT WHERE? YOUR SOLARIUM IS FILLED WITH ORCHIDS!

THE WIDOW'S WALK— THERE'S LOADS OF ROOM!

ACTUALLY, DEAR, PROP 215 HAS A LOT OF SUPPORT FROM RESPECTABLE QUARTERS. UNFORTUNATELY, IT'S OPPOSED BY OUR AMBITIOUS ATTORNEY GENERAL, DAN LUNGREN.

DANNY LUNGREN? WHY, I'VE KNOWN HIS FAMILY FOR YEARS!

THEN YOU SHOULD KNOW HE HAS A HEART LIKE A PEACH PIT! HE WANTS VERY ILL PEOPLE TO CHOOSE BETWEEN PAIN AND LAW-BREAKING.

OH, DEAR, DEAR, DEAR...

LET ME TALK TO HIS MOTHER.

COULD YOU, DEAR? I'M GETTING TIRED OF PAYING STREET PRICES.

141

ANYWAY, SINCE I WAS IN TOWN TO GIVE THIS LECTURE, I THOUGHT I'D STOP BY!

IT'S GREAT TO SEE YOU, JOANIE! WELCOME BACK!

ARE YOU SURE YOU'RE NOT BUSY?

NOT AT ALL, I JUST FINISHED UP MY WEEKLY DISCUSSION GROUP!

REALLY? WHAT WAS IT ON?

WELL, ACTUALLY, THE MOST SERIOUS CRISIS NOW FACING MY CONGREGATION...

A CRISIS OF SPIRIT?

UM...NO, PARKING. BUT THAT'S ON THE LIST.

LET ME SHOW YOU AROUND, JOANIE! THERE'VE BEEN LOTS OF CHANGES AT THE LITTLE CHURCH OF WALDEN!

THE OLD HOUSE IS USED FOR OUR SPIRITUAL WELLNESS SEMINARS AND VARIOUS 12-STEP RECOVERY PROGRAMS...

IN THE NEW WINGS, WE HAVE A FOOD COURT, A FITNESS CENTER, AND OUR INTERPRETIVE DANCE STUDIOS.

UM...WHERE DO PEOPLE WORSHIP?

ON OUR WEB SITE. KEEPS THE HEATING BILLS DOWN.

"WELCOME TO THE LIT-TLE CHURCH OF WALDEN WEB SITE."

PRETTY GREAT, HUH? IT'S THE PERFECT PRAYER PLATFORM FOR BUSY CHRIS-TIANS...

BY CONGREGATING ON-LINE, PEOPLE CAN CUSTOMIZE THEIR WORSHIPING NEEDS. THERE'S VIRTUAL COMMUNION, OF COURSE, AND INTERACTIVE BIBLE STORIES...

AND THIS IS MY SERMON PAGE, WHICH SITE VISITORS LITERALLY FLOCK TO! THIS SECTION MUST DRAW TWO MILLION HITS A DAY.

TWO MILLION?

EASILY. I MEAN, I DON'T KNOW THAT FOR SURE, BUT IT STANDS TO REASON.

...AND THIS PAGE IS OUR GEN X REACH-OUT CENTER. WE CALL IT "ROCK THE FLOCK."

IT HAS A LARGE CHAT HALL WHERE THE UNCHURCHED YOUNG CAN GET DOWN WITH THEIR PEERS...

THIS IS THE CONGREGATION OF TOMORROW, REFUGEES FROM A DEEPLY SECULAR WORLD WHO ACCESS US TO RESTORE VALUES AND SPIRITUALITY TO THEIR LIVES.

I SEE YOU'RE ACCEPTING LIQUOR ADS.

WELL, I FOUGHT THAT.

142

IT'S NICE OF YOU TO DRIVE ME TO MY LEC-TURE, SCOT...

NO PROBLEM. I JUST HOPE YOUR HUSBAND WON'T MIND!

MIND? WHAT DO YOU MEAN?

WELL, DIDN'T YOU TELL HIM ABOUT US? THAT WE WERE ONCE LINKED?

MAYBE YOU BETTER FILL ME IN FIRST.

UM...I'M NOT SAYING IT WAS A BIG DEAL OR ANYTHING.

WOW...BEING IN THIS AUDITORIUM SURE BRINGS BACK MEMORIES, DOESN'T IT, JOANIE?

UM...NOT REALLY. HAVE I BEEN HERE BEFORE?

ON OUR BIG DATE! WE CAME HERE TO HEAR JEB MAGRUDER, THE WATERGATE CONSPIRATOR!

WE DID?

HE WAS SO... SO CONTRITE, MOVING US BOTH TO TEARS. LATER, I COMFORTED YOU, HOLDING YOU IN MY ARMS...

OH, SCOT! YOU MOST CERTAINLY DID NOT!

WELL, I MIGHT HAVE. HOW DO YOU KNOW? YOU DON'T RE-MEMBER.

I ALREADY HAVE ENOUGH THINGS TO REGRET, THANK YOU VERY MUCH.

I'LL JUST SAY IN CONCLUDING THAT IT HAS BEEN A PRIVILEGE TO SERVE IN THIS ADMINISTRATION...

THE PRESIDENT'S CORE BELIEF THAT GOVERNMENT CAN IMPROVE THE LIVES OF ORDINARY PEOPLE IS THE ANIMATING SPIRIT BEHIND ALL OF US ON HIS TEAM...

WITH THE SUPPORT OF THE AMERICAN PEOPLE, THE PRESIDENT MAY WELL LEAD US ACROSS THAT FAMOUS BRIDGE AND INTO THE PAGES OF HISTORY! THANK YOU VERY MUCH!

OKAY, WHY DON'T I TAKE A FEW QUESTIONS... YES, SIR?

YEAH, IS CLINTON GOING TO BE INDICTED?

YES, THE LADY IN THE BACK...

YEAH, I HAVE A QUESTION ON WHITEWATER...

BUT FIRST, I WANT TO THANK YOU AND THE ATTORNEY GENERAL FOR APPOINTING ALL THOSE SPECIAL PROSECUTORS...

I WAS TOO YOUNG FOR WATERGATE, SO I'VE NEVER SEEN A PRESIDENT IN SERIOUS LEGAL TROUBLE BEFORE! IT'S **VERY** EXCITING!

MA'AM, WE DIDN'T ACT JUST SO YOUR AGE GROUP COULD...

SO WHEN DO YOU ARREST HIM? HOW DOES THAT WORK?

143

... SO, NO, WE DON'T FEEL THE WHITE HOUSE HAS BEEN "CRIPPLED"!

MS. CAUCUS, WILL YOU BE APPOINTING A SPECIAL PROSECUTOR FOR THE DNC?

UM...WELL, WE'RE CURRENTLY REVIEWING THE DNC ALLEGATIONS...

GOOD! I MEAN, SOMETHING REALLY SMELLS THERE!

OKAY, IF THERE ARE NO OTHER...

JOAN, HOW MANY SPECIAL PROSECUTORS ARE INVESTIGATING CLINTON? I SAY 19, BUT MY FRIEND SAYS 21!

WELL, YOU'RE **BOTH** WRONG...

IT'S 20, ISN'T IT? I **KNEW** IT! I **SAID** 20!

YEAH, WHAT'S GOING ON WITH THE PAULA JONES CASE?

WELL, THE SUPREME COURT WILL BE HEARING ORAL ARGUMENTS IN JANUARY...

ORAL ARGUMENTS? THAT SOUNDS SORT OF OBSCENE ALL BY ITSELF!

WHAT AN **APPALLING** COMMENT, YOUNG MAN!

IT IS **PRECISELY** THAT KIND OF UTTER DISRESPECT AND INCIVILITY THAT HAS MADE PUBLIC SERVICE SO INHOSPITABLE FOR PEOPLE WHO GENUINELY WANT TO MAKE A **DIFFERENCE** IN GOVERNMENT!

WHATEVER. SO DID CLINTON FLASH HER?

WHAT?

YOU DON'T HAVE TO TAKE THIS, JOANIE...

144

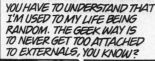

148

150

153

HEY, BABE...

WHATCHA WORKING ON?

1001...

10010010000111010f7
11000%^·¶§∞100∞§¶99
0001///¨§0011§10¢¨//11
00010111//¨†110000¶¶8.

YOU KNOW, THERE'S NOTHING SEXIER THAN A GIRL GEEK ON A BIG CODING RUN.

1001//.

BOY, YOU WERE ON A TECHIE **TEAR** THIS MORNING, KIM...

WAS I?

WHEN I'M HACKING A CHUNK OF CODE, I TEND TO TUNE OUT, TO GET IN THE ZONE...

WHEN I WAS IN COLLEGE I USED TO FLASH ON COOL IDEAS IN THE SHOWER. I'D JUMP OUT, RUN TO MY P.C., AND TYPE IN THE NUDE FOR **HOURS!**

I... I WOULD HAVE TRANSFERRED TO SEE THAT.

REALLY? I WAS AT M.I.T. — MY HOUSEMATES NEVER NOTICED.

ANYWAY, I SHOULD HAVE THE SITE UP WITHIN A WEEK!

SO...UM... WHAT THEN? BACK TO PARIS?

YES, THAT'S ONE POSSIBLE SCENARIO. ANOTHER IS THAT YOU QUIT YOUR JOB, MARKET A NEW WEB BROWSER I'LL DESIGN, WE MAKE MILLIONS, GET MARRIED, AND MOVE INTO A HIGH-TECH PLEASURE PALACE OVERLOOKING PUGET SOUND!

HE'S THINKING, HE'S THINKING...

NO, I'M MIDDLE-AGED. I NEVER JOKE ABOUT THE FUTURE.

KIM, I DON'T LIKE TO TRIVIALIZE COMMITMENTS...

MIKE, I'M SERIOUS!

A HIGH-TECH PLEASURE PALACE IS SERIOUS?

OKAY, MAYBE NOT THAT PART...

WHAT I **AM** SERIOUS ABOUT IS YOU AND ME STARTING OUR OWN COMPANY AND MAKING A LIFE TOGETHER!

WHAT ABOUT ALEX?

SHE CAN RUN THE COMPANY.

WE HAVE TO MOVE THE WATER- FALL OVER ABOUT SIX FEET, BUT YOU GET THE GENERAL PICTURE...

BASICALLY, WHAT I'M HAVING BUILT HERE IS THE MOST COSTLY, AMBITIOUS, FEATURE-RICH PRI- VATE RESIDENCE IN ALL SEATTLE!

THAT'S WHERE YOU COME IN. I'M GOING TO NEED OUTDOOR SCULPTURE EVERY BIT AS MAS- SIVE, MUSCULAR AND BRUTALLY COOL AS THE HOUSE ITSELF!

NO PROBLEM. NONE!

WELL, WE HAVE TO TALK DE- POSIT.

I CALL IT "THE COTTAGE"! IT'LL BE 10,000 SQ. FT. BIGGER AND $25 MILLION MORE COSTLY THAN BILL GATES' PLACE!

UNFORTUNATELY, IT WON'T BE DONE BEFORE GATES UNVEILS HIS HOUSE IN THE SPRING. MY ONLY HOPE IS HE'LL GIVE HIS GUESTS A LAKEFRONT TOUR...

IF HE DOES, I WANT TO HOSE HIM! I WANT TO HAVE AN EXTER- IOR ART FEATURE IN PLACE THAT WILL **SMOKE** ANYTHING HE'S GOT!

HMM...TOUGH AS- SIGNMENT. EVIL EMPIRE ART IS COOL–VERY COOL.

IF ONLY I COULD MAKE THESE NUM- BERS WORK!

ADD A ZERO.

OKAY, THIS IS WHERE I WANT THE MAIN ART INSTALLATION...

IT'S GOT TO **DOMINATE** THE LAKEFRONT, JUST **RULE** IT! IT HAS TO BE COMPLETELY IN THE FACE OF ANYONE WITHIN A **MILE!**

WHEW! THAT'S A LOT OF DISTRESSED STEEL AND CONCRETE!

I HOPE YOU'RE NOT OFFENDED BY SUCH AN UN- DERTAKING, MS. DOONESBURY...

NOT AT ALL. A LOT OF GREAT ART IS COMMIS- SIONED OUT OF SPITE.

OH, THAT'S RIGHT– YOU USED TO WORK FOR TRUMP.

CAN YOU BELIEVE IT? MY THIRD COMMISSION IN A **MONTH!** ZEKE, I'M THE ART PRINCESS OF PUGET SOUND!

DO YOU KNOW HOW VALIDAT- ING THAT IS, HOW EMPOWERING? TO KNOW THAT MY ART HAS BEEN EMBRACED BY THE HIGH LORDS OF CYBERTOWN?

YOU CAN'T WAIT TO RUB MIKE'S NOSE IN IT, CAN YOU?

WANT TO SWING BY NOW? THINK HE'D BE HOME?

LOOK, B.D., YOU ASK ANY KID IN THE REAL WORLD WHETHER IT'S EASIER TO GET ALCOHOL OR POT, AND HE'LL TELL YOU POT! AND EVERY STUDY SUPPORTS THAT!

SO IF CIVIL REGULATION WORKS BETTER, THEN WHAT EXACTLY IS THE **POINT** OF SPENDING BILLIONS ON PROHIBITION?

DOES HE USUALLY THINK THIS HARD?

NO, THIS IS NEW.

JOBS!

YOU KNOW WHAT **REALLY** DISGUSTS ME, HARRIS? THE FACT THAT THE VOTERS WERE SO EASILY DUPED BY YOU PEOPLE!

WHO SAYS THEY WERE DUPED, B.D.? WHO SAYS THEY HAVE TO KEEP BELIEVING IN A COSTLY, FAILED, IN-HUMANE POLICY OF PROHIBITION?

HARRIS, IF PEOPLE REALLY UNDERSTOOD THIS LAW, THERE'S NO **WAY** THEY... THEY...

WHAT'S THAT?

BASIL.

SAGE! WE AGREED I'D BE SAGE!

IT'S **POT**, ISN'T IT? YOU'RE GROWING **POT** ON MY SUN-DECK!

YEAH. IT'S FOR AN AIDS PATIENT IN THE VALLEY.

HARRIS, IF YOU DON'T HAVE A DOCTOR'S NOTE, CONSIDER YOUR-SELF BUSTED!

WELL, SEE, THAT'S A PERFECT EXAMPLE OF WHAT I WAS TALK-ING ABOUT!

I'M NOT HURTING ANYONE! IN FACT, I'M TRYING TO HELP SOMEONE! BUT YOU'RE HAPPY TO INCARCERATE ME AT HUGE TAXPAYER EXPENSE! WHAT PUB-LIC GOOD WOULD THAT SERVE?

B.D., IF YOU AR-REST OUR NANNY, I'LL KILL YOU!

AW, BOOP-SIE!

HEY, THAT REMINDS ME—I NEED A RAISE.

WELL, THIS JUST PROVES WHAT I WAS SAYING—PROP 215 IS REALLY A-BOUT LEGALIZATION!

RELAX, B.D.— YOUR JOB IS SECURE...

DRUGS HAVE BECOME SO POLI-TICIZED, IT'LL TAKE AT LEAST 20 MORE YEARS OF VIOLENT CRIME, WRECKED LIVES, AND WASTED BILLIONS BEFORE PRO-HIBITION IS ABANDONED!

20 YEARS?

AT LEAST.

THAT DOES GET ME TO RETIRE-MENT...

MY POINT EXACTLY.

162

165

166

168

172

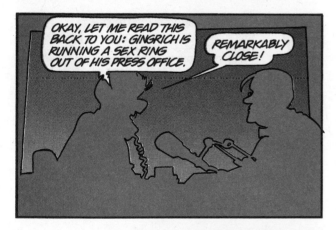

174

176

IN SEATTLE, LIFE GOES ON.

MIKE, WERE YOU ABLE TO GET TO CIRCUIT CITY?

YUP. I GOT YOUR MODEM.

I ALSO PICKED UP A 12-FOOT SCUZZY CABLE FOR THE SCANNER. I'VE GOT YOU ALL SET UP NOW IN THE GARAGE.

OH, BY THE WAY— THEY'RE ENGAGED.

LIKE BLISS.

TELL ME ABOUT IT.

HAVE YOU TOLD ANYONE YET ABOUT OUR ENGAGEMENT?

NOPE. I WANT TO EXPERIENCE IT FIRST AS A SECRET.

NO KIDDING? ME, TOO.

COOL. THEN WE WON'T TELL A SOUL.

WHY, ARE YOU AFRAID YOUR FRIENDS WILL LAUGH?

A LITTLE. YOU **ARE** IN MARKETING.

177

HI, BERNIE, WHAT'S UP?... CONGRATULATIONS FOR WHAT?... HEY, HOW'D YOU HEAR? WE HAVEN'T TOLD **ANYONE** YET!

WHAT'S THAT? YOU SAY YOU RECEIVED AN ANONYMOUS E-MAIL ANNOUNCEMENT FROM SOMEONE WITH ATROCIOUS SPELLING?

OKAY, I ADMIT I'M THE LOGICAL SUSPECT.

YEAH, LEMME CALL YOU BACK, BERN...

ALEX...

I'M SORRY, POP, BUT THE NEWS ABOUT YOU AND KIM WAS TOO NEATO-FRITO TO KEEP TO MYSELF!

I COULDN'T DECIDE WHO TO TELL FIRST, SO I JUST E-MAILED EVERYONE IN OUR COMPUTER ADDRESS BOOK!

EVERYONE? YOU E-MAILED EVERYONE?

UH...YEAH, IS THAT BAD?

WHAT? HE'S **MARRYING** THAT...THAT TEENAGER?

THIS IS ABOUT SEX, I GUARANTEE IT.

YOU HAVE TO UNDERSTAND, ALEX— MARRIAGE IS A VERY PRIVATE DECISION. I WANTED TO SAVOR IT...

I'M SORRY, DADDY. IT'S JUST THAT A LITTLE GIRL'S JOY IS A HARD THING TO CONTAIN...

BUT SO EASY TO SNUFF OUT!

OH, KNOCK IT OFF.

HEY, FUTURE STEP-MOMSTER— STILL WORKING ON THE GUEST LIST?

UH-HUH. I'VE GOT IT DOWN TO UNDER 300.

300? YOU KNOW 300 PEOPLE?

YUP. NOW I'M ORGANIZING THEM IN CATEGORIES SO I CAN PRIORITIZE THEM.

CATEGORIES? WHAT SORT OF CATEGORIES?

OKAY, WELL, LIKE THIS COLUMN IS OLD BOYFRIENDS...

WOW! DADDY BEAT OUT ALL THOSE GUYS?

HOLD IT!

178

BOYFRIENDS? YOU WANT TO INVITE BOYFRIENDS?

FORMER BOYFRIENDS! THEY'RE MY BUDS NOW, MY TRIBE!

I UNDERSTAND, BUT THIS IS OUR WEDDING, KIM!

SO? I DON'T SEE WHAT THE BIG DEAL IS.

LOOK, I JUST THINK WE SHOULD HAVE SOME GROUND RULES FOR THE GUEST LIST, OKAY?

LIKE WHAT?

WELL, LIKE, NO PEOPLE WHO'VE SLEPT WITH THE BRIDE.

OH, GREAT! SO WE ONLY INVITE YOUR FRIENDS?

MICHAEL, I REALLY DON'T SEE WHY YOU'RE HAVING SUCH A PROBLEM WITH MY INVITING A FEW MALE FRIENDS TO THE WEDDING...

YOU DON'T?

NO. I MEAN, YOU'VE GOT ALL THESE WOMEN ON YOUR LIST...

LIKE WHO?

WELL, LIKE, WHO'S THIS JOANIE CAUCUS?

UM...MY FORMER MOTHER-IN-LAW.

OH! HOW SPECIAL! SHALL WE SEAT HER AT THE HEAD TABLE?

YOU'D LIKE TO INVITE YOUR FORMER **MOTHER-IN-LAW?** I DON'T EVEN WANT TO **KNOW** WHAT THAT'S ABOUT!

HEY, IT'S NO CRAZIER THAN INVITING OLD BOYFRIENDS FROM YOUR "TRIBE"!

OKAY, OKAY, LET'S MAKE A DEAL...

IN THE INTERESTS OF PEACE, WE WON'T INVITE **ANYONE** ASSOCIATED WITH OUR RESPECTIVE PAST ROMANTIC HISTORIES, OKAY?

NOT OKAY!

WITH ONE EXCEPTION, OF COURSE.

YOU KNOW, POPSTER, YOU GUYS OUGHT TO GET MARRIED ON THE SPACE NEEDLE! AND HAVE FIREWORKS OR SOMETHING!

OR HAVE IT AT A CYBER CAFE, SO ALL THE GUESTS CAN PLAY ON THE WEB! OR AT SIT & SPIN, WHERE EVERYONE CAN DANCE AND DO THEIR LAUNDRY AFTER THE CEREMONY!

UM... ACTUALLY, WE WERE THINKING OF A CHURCH.

A CHURCH? WHAT DO PEOPLE DO AT A CHURCH?

GET MARRIED.

PERFECT!

179

NOW **THAT'S** A SCULPTURE, MAN! WHAT'S IT MEAN?

IT'S ABOUT HUMANITY'S FAILED SEARCH FOR CORPOREAL STASIS.

WELL, I THOUGHT SO.

IT'S ALSO ABOUT THE NEW POST-HARDWARE PARADIGM, WHICH, OF COURSE, INFORMED MY CHOICE OF MATERIAL...

...DISCARDED EXERCISE MACHINES.

YOU'RE SCARY, MAN.

SO HOW'RE YOU GOING TO GET THIS SUCKER OUT TO THE CLIENT'S ESTATE?

WELL, I'M NOT SURE...

HOW ABOUT GETTING A HEAVY CRANE AND PUTTING IT ON A BARGE AND JUST FLOATING IT OVER?

GOOD IDEA. YOU KNOW ANYTHING ABOUT OPERATING A BARGE OR HEAVY CRANE?

NO, BUT HELL, HOW HARD COULD IT BE?

YOU ARE **SO** CAN-DO, ZEKE! I CAN'T BELIEVE I MARRIED SOMEONE ELSE!

180

OKAY, FOLKS, TIME FOR KIM'S SEATTLE TRIBE TO LOG ON! GIRLFRIEND, YOUR OLD HOUSEMATES HAVE WRITTEN A POEM FOR YOU...!

UH-OH.

HERE GOES..."WHEN KIM ANNOUNCED THAT SHE'D STRUCK GOLD, WE GAVE HER GRIEF 'CAUSE MIKE'S SO OLD!"

"IT'S CLEAR THAT THOSE WHO TEASE HER DREAD... MARRIAGE TO A GEEZERHEAD!"

HA, HA, HA!

HEH, HEH.

WAIT, WAIT, THERE'S MORE!

OKAY, I WANT TO MAKE A TOAST, TOO, OKAY?

SURE, SWEETHEART.

OKAY, I WANT TO TOAST THE COOLEST GIRL GEEK AND THE PHATTEST PAPA I KNOW...

TO KIMBO KARUMBA AND THE AMAZING DAD-O-RAMA POPMEISTER!

TO KIMBO KARUMBA AND THE AMAZING DAD-O-RAMA POPMEISTER!

WHICH ONE AM I?

HEY, EVERYONE — COULD I HAVE YOUR ATTENTION, PLEASE?

IN A FEW MINUTES, WE'LL BE PUTTING IN. THE BUS BACK TO THE HOTEL WILL BE PARKED IN FRONT OF THE TERMINAL.

MY SWEET BRIDE AND I WILL BE TAKING OFF, OF COURSE, SO I JUST WANT TO THANK YOU ALL FOR COMING SUCH A LONG WAY TO SHARE THIS DAY WITH US!

YOU GUYS ARE THE BEST! I REALLY...

EXCUSE ME, MAN. I DIDN'T GET A CHANCE TO KISS THE BRIDE.

WANT SOME RICE TO THROW, MAN?

WHAT DO YOU THINK, ZEKE?

SURE IS ONE OF THOSE DAYS FILLED WITH "WHAT IF'S", ISN'T IT, MAN?

HOW DO YOU MEAN?

WELL, LIKE, WHAT IF TWO YEARS AGO, I'D DRIVEN THROUGH SEATTLE INSTEAD OF ASPEN? YOU'D STILL BE MARRIED TO MIKE, AND I MIGHT'VE BEEN THE ONE MARRIED TO A TOTAL BABE!

LIFE'S FUNNY, ISN'T IT?

YEAH. FOR INSTANCE, WHO KNEW I'D BE DUMPING YOU TODAY?

184

SO TELL ME WHAT YOU TWO HAVE GOT PLANNED FOR VIETNAM!

WELL, WE'RE GOING TO GO EXPLORE THE HUE AREA AND SEE IF WE CAN FIND MY BIRTH PARENTS' GRAVES...

WE'RE ALSO GOING TO TRY TO LOCATE ANY SURVIVING RELATIVES, ALTHOUGH I THINK MOST OF THEM LIKELY DIED DURING TET.

HAS THAT GOT HONEYMOON WRITTEN ALL OVER IT OR WHAT?

WELL, NOW, I'M SURE KIM'LL PACK SOME NEGLIGEE, RIGHT, DEAR?

ALEX? WHY THE LONG FACE, CHILD?

DADS AND KIM ARE LEAVING, TONIGHT. I'M GOING TO GET STUCK FOR TWO WEEKS WITH SOME LAME BABYSITTER.

NO, YOU'RE NOT, DEAR. I'M LOOKING AFTER YOU.

YOU ARE? YEAAA! I GET TO HANG WITH THE NOTORIOUS GRAMMY D!

IT'S OKAY IF I CALL YOU THE NOTORIOUS GRAMMY D, ISN'T IT?

HEAVENS, DEAR, I WOULDN'T KNOW. IS IT DISRESPECTFUL?

MIKE, I'M SO WIRED ABOUT THIS TRIP I CAN BARELY BREATHE.

UNDERSTANDABLY. DOING A ROOTS SEARCH ON YOUR HONEYMOON IS PRETTY INTENSE...

THE TIMING IS RIGHT, THOUGH. BEFORE BEGINNING A NEW CHAPTER OF YOUR LIFE, YOU NEED TO COME TO TERMS WITH THE PAST.

IT'S FUNNY HOW WEDDINGS ALWAYS BRING THINGS TO A HEAD. AND NOT JUST FOR THE HAPPY COUPLE!

CASE IN POINT.

WHAT HAVE YOU DONE WITH MARK?

LIKE IT? I DID IT FOR YOU.

ANYWAY, THE WEDDING JUST GOT ME THINKING ABOUT NEW BEGINNINGS, FRESH STARTS. IT WAS TIME FOR A CHANGE.

AS YOU KNOW, I'VE NEVER REALLY THOUGHT THROUGH WHAT IT MEANS TO BE AN IDENTIFIABLE GAY MAN. I'VE NEVER ADDRESSED KEY FASHION AND GROOMING ISSUES, MY NEW HAIRCUT IS A FIRST STEP.

MARK, I WANT YOU TO LISTEN TO ME VERY CAREFULLY.

SURE. WHAT'S UP?

GET HELP.

WHAT— YOU MEAN LIKE A PERSONAL STYLIST?

SAIGON.

MADAM, I'VE DONE A COMPLETE DOCUMENT SEARCH OF YOUR CASE...

AS YOU KNOW, YOUR PARENTS PERISHED AT THE END OF THE WAR, ALONG WITH YOUR SISTER.

YOUR GRANDPARENTS DIED DURING THE TET OFFENSIVE, ONE UNCLE WAS KILLED BY AIR PIRATES, THE OTHER BY PUPPETS! SO I'M AFRAID ALL YOUR RELATIVES IN HUE ARE DEAD!

DEAD! DEAD! EVERYONE DEAD!

HOW ABOUT MUSEUMS? ANY GOOD MUSEUMS IN THE AREA?

MISS HAI, ARE YOU SURE NONE OF MY FAMILY SURVIVED THE WAR?

NONE OF YOUR IMMEDIATE FAMILY. YOU DO HAVE A SECOND COUSIN WHO'S STILL ALIVE...

I DO?

HER NAME IS DO TRANG. SHE LIVES OUTSIDE OF HO CHI MINH CITY.

WHAT'S SHE DO?

SHE WORKS FOR NIKE.

REALLY? COOL!

UH-OH...

187

...AND MIKE'S NOW OFF LOOKING AT THE WAR MUSEUM!

SO HOW'S YOUR SEARCH FOR FAMILY GOING, HON?

WELL, THAT'S WHY I CALLED, MOM. NOBODY SEEMS TO HAVE SURVIVED EXCEPT A SECOND COUSIN NAMED DO TRANG...

SHE WORKS IN A NIKE FACTORY. I THOUGHT I'D GO OUT THERE TODAY...

A NIKE FACTORY? YOUR COUSIN WORKS IN A NIKE FACTORY?

YUP. SO I NEED DADDY'S SNEAKER SIZE.

HOLD ON, I'LL PUT HIM ON...

(EXCUSE ME, MR. HUNG— I'M AFRAID WE HAVE ANOTHER VISITOR...)

(WHERE FROM THIS TIME?)

(AMERICA. SHE SAYS SHE HAS A COUSIN WHO'S A NIKE EMPLOYEE.)

(YEAH, RIGHT. SHE'S GOT TO BE FROM ONE OF THOSE DAMN HUMAN RIGHTS GROUPS! STICK WITH HER!)

(DON'T WORRY, BOSS, I WILL...)

(FORTUNATELY, SHE DOESN'T SPEAK VIETNAMESE!)

(WELL, A TINY BIT. I TOOK ONE CREDIT.)

DESPITE WHAT YOU MIGHT HAVE HEARD, MISS, THERE IS A SPECIAL FEELING HERE AT NIKE FACTORY #5! IT'S THAT FEELING THAT EMPLOYEES GET...

47 B

JUST DO IT!

...WHEN THEY KNOW THEY'RE WORKING FOR SOMETHING BIGGER THAN JUST THEMSELVES!

NIKE

WHAT'S THAT OUT IN THE YARD?

CASE IN POINT. IT'S A SHRINE. ALL WORKERS ARE ALLOWED FIVE MINUTES A DAY TO WORSHIP.

NIKE

BUDDHA?

JORDAN.

(HEY, NUMBER 237, SHIFT 2! YOU'VE GOT A VISITOR!)

JUS DO IT

(A VISITOR? WHO WOULD VISIT ME?)

(SHE SAYS SHE'S YOUR COUSIN.)

HI!

(MY COUSIN? BUT I DON'T RECOGNIZE HER...)

(OF COURSE YOU DON'T, SIMPLETON! SHE'S FROM AMERICA!)

NIKE

(AMERICA? HAS SHE COME TO FREE ME FROM THIS HELL-HOLE?)

SHE SAYS SHE HAS TO GET BACK TO WORK.

YEAH, RIGHT. WHAT'S (HELL-HOLE) MEAN?

188

(SHE WANTS TO KNOW HOW YOU ARE TREATED HERE IN OUR NIKE FACTORY. YOU ARE TREATED VERY WELL, CORRECT?)

(DON'T MAKE ME LAUGH! I'M PAID LESS PER DAY THAN THE COST OF THREE SIMPLE MEALS. I'VE LOST WEIGHT, AND SUFFER FROM HEADACHES AND FATIGUE!)

(I'VE BEEN SUBJECTED TO VERBAL AND PHYSICAL ABUSE, AND GET ONLY ONE BATHROOM BREAK A DAY!)

(UH-HUH...)

GOOD NEWS— ALL IS WELL! WHY TAKE NOTES?

I WANT TO LOOK UP A FEW WORDS.

NI N

(NIKE SIGNED THE NEW ANTI-SWEATSHOP AGREEMENT, WHICH GUARANTEES MINIMUM WAGE...)

SHE'S THRILLED BY NIKE'S COMMITMENT TO A FAIR WAGE!

(BUT MINIMUM WAGE IS NOT THE SAME AS A LIVING WAGE! ON $1.60 A DAY, I CANNOT EVEN AFFORD TO EAT!)

ALTHOUGH SHE STILL HAS TO WATCH THE FAMILY FOOD BUDGET CAREFULLY!

(PLEASE— TELL THE WORLD WHAT YOU'VE SEEN HERE TODAY!)

SHE IMPLORES YOU NOT TO REPORT YOUR UNFOUNDED SUSPICIONS ABOUT THIS FACILITY.

WHY NOT?

NI

(OUR LIVES ARE IN YOUR HANDS!)

SHE'S WORRIED YOU'LL EMBARRASS TIGER WOODS.

HOW LONG HAVE YOU BEEN TRANSLATING HERE?

190

LISTEN, MIKE, I KNOW THAT TRENT CAN BE HARD TO TAKE...

BUT WE NEED HIS TALENT TO BE COMPETITIVE. HE REALLY IS THE BEST AT WHAT HE DOES!

I'M SURE IN TIME YOU'LL GET USED TO HAVING HIM AROUND. HE'S ACTUALLY PRETTY LOW MAINTENANCE...

HEY, MAN. MIND IF I USE YOUR CAN?

YES!

KIMSTER, WHO'S THE GUY OUT IN THE GARAGE WITH POP?

HIS NAME'S TRENT, ALEX...

I HIRED HIM AS LEAD DESIGNER FOR OUR NEW COMPANY...

YOUR DADDY'S A LITTLE UNHAPPY THAT TRENT'S AN OLD BOYFRIEND OF MINE, BUT HE'S PROMISED TO GIVE HIM A CHANCE.

SO YOU DON'T MIND THAT I'VE SEEN HER NAKED?

I DIDN'T SAY THAT.

JEREMY CAVENDISH CAME BY TO SEE ME YESTERDAY. HE'S WORRIED ABOUT LACEY...

WHY? SHE STILL WON'T GO OUT WITH HIM?

ON THE CONTRARY— THEY GO OUT EVERY NIGHT...

IT'S ALWAYS A DISASTER, OF COURSE, BUT WHEN JEREMY CALLS UP THE NEXT DAY TO APOLOGIZE, SHE DOESN'T EVEN RECALL GOING OUT WITH HIM!

THAT'S NOT GOOD.

WELL, HE'S TORN. HE **IS** GETTING MORE DATES.

YOU KNOW, LACEY MUST BE CLOSE TO WHAT—90? IT'D BE ODD IF SHE **WEREN'T** A LITTLE FORGETFUL...

WELL, EXACTLY. BUT JEREMY'S SURE IT'S DEMENTIA...

AND IF IT IS, SHE SHOULDN'T BE IN THE POSITION OF RESPONSIBILITY SHE'S IN. SOMEONE'S GOING TO HAVE TO PERSUADE HER TO RESIGN HER HOUSE SEAT.

HMM... THAT DOESN'T SEEM FAIR SOMEHOW...

WHAT DO YOU MEAN?

SHOULDN'T STROM THURMOND HAVE TO GO FIRST?

NO, THAT'S THE SENATE— IT'S A MUSEUM OVER THERE.

WHY, JERE-MY...

SORRY TO BARGE IN, MRS. REDFERN, BUT HAVE YOU TALKED TO MRS. D YET?

NOT YET, BUT I MADE AN APPOINTMENT FOR THIS AFTERNOON...

WELL, I HOPE I'M WRONG ABOUT THE ALZHEIMER'S DISEASE...

IF NOT, I WANT TO DO WHATEVER I CAN TO HELP WITH HER CARE. I WANT TO BE THERE FOR HER. I'D EVEN BE WILLING TO MOVE IN!

I DON'T THINK THAT'LL BE NECESSARY, JEREMY...

NO TROUBLE AT ALL. I'M BEING EVICTED THIS WEEK, SO THE TIMING'S PERFECT!

JOANIE CAUCUS HERE TO SEE YOU, MRS. DAVENPORT!

SPLENDID! SEND HER IN!

GO RIGHT IN, JOANIE.

THANKS, CYNTHIA.

OH, AMBER? ONE MORE THING...

YES, MRS. DAVENPORT?

WHO'S HERE TO SEE ME?

JOANIE CAUCUS.

WHO'S AMBER?

CYNTHIA, DID I JUST HEAR LACEY CALL YOU "AMBER"?

YES, AMBER ANSWERS THE MAIL. LACEY'S BEEN GETTING US CONFUSED.

HAS SHE BEEN CONFUSED A LOT LATELY? NOT QUITE HERSELF?

THAT'S PUTTING IT MILDLY.

HOW SO?

WELL, LIKE, SHE KEEPS TRYING TO CUT SOCIAL SECURITY.

HMM... THAT'S ONLY CRAZY, NOT DEMENTED.

COME IN, DEAR— IT'S LOVELY TO SEE YOU!

HOW ARE YOU, LACEY?

ME? NEVER BETTER, DEAR!

WELL, YOU LOOK WONDERFUL!

THANK YOU, DEAR! YOU'RE ALSO LOOKING QUITE...QUITE...

QUITE?

FAMILIAR.

SMASHING!

WHY, THANK YOU!

You've BEEN to see a doctor? — **Yes, Jeremy was right about the Alzheimer's...**

The good news is that I'm in the earliest stages. The doctor was very encouraging.

What'd he say, exactly? — **Who?**

Your doctor. — **HE told you? Why, that's HORRIBLY unethical!**

I don't know, dear—I'm having a lot of trouble accepting my condition.

You want to know the worst thing about this dreadful disease? — **What?**

It's... it's...

:SIGH:... I keep forgetting the point I want to make. — **I'll bet that was it.**

You know, Lacey, even if you weren't ill, you are 90 — don't you deserve a break?

I mean, you've served non-stop for 20 years now, not including your brief resignation... — **I resigned? When?**

Um... in 1991. You resigned on principle. — **On principle? Gracious! Which one?**

You... you really don't recall? — **I'll bet it was over tidiness. I'm a bear about tidiness!**

Lacey, I've been talking to some of your staff, and they're a little worried about your ability to manage your job...

They say you've been prone to forgetfulness, lack of focus, mood swings... — **Well, of course they'd say that...**

They're all jockeying for POWER! Don't you see? They want my PARKING SPACE! Well, I won't STAND for it!

...and occasional paranoia. — **Nonsense, dear! I'm from a VERY safe district!**

LACEY, YOU'VE BEEN A GREAT LEGISLATOR—AN INSPIRATION TO SO MANY OF US...

IT'S VERY HARD FOR ME TO SAY THIS, BUT IT MAY BE TIME FOR YOU TO LET GO, TO STEP DOWN WITH YOUR FULL DIGNITY AND REPUTATION INTACT.

I HAVE TO GO NOW, BUT PROMISE ME YOU'LL THINK ABOUT IT, OKAY?

I PROMISE, DEAR.

NICE TO SEE YOU, LACEY.

YOU, TOO, DEAR.

I WONDER WHAT SHE WANTED.

HOW'D IT GO, JOANIE?

WELL, I'M NOT SURE...

MOST OF THE TIME SHE WAS HER OLD SELF, CYNTHIA. MAYBE IT *IS* TOO SOON TO BE TALKING ABOUT HER STEPPING DOWN...

OH, AMBER?

UH... YES, MRS. DAVENPORT?

I THINK JOANIE STOLE MY CHAIR.

CHECK BEHIND YOUR DESK, MA'AM.

~SIGH~

195

KIM? YOU SEEN MY RUNNING SHOES?

YOUR RUNNING SHOES? YOU MEAN THE ONES MADE BY EXHAUSTED WORKERS DURING FORCED OVERTIME?

THE ONES MADE BY THE COMPANY WHOSE NAME HAS BECOME SYNONYMOUS WITH CHRONIC VIOLATIONS OF MINIMUM WAGE LAWS?

I'M NEVER GOING TO SEE MY SHOES AGAIN, AM I?

I HID MINE.

PORSTER? WHAT'S THE DEAL WITH KIMBALINA AND NIKE?

WELL, SHE VISITED ONE OF THEIR FACTORIES IN VIETNAM...

KIM WAS VERY UPSET BY HOW NIKE TREATED ITS WORKERS, SO SHE DECIDED TO JOIN THE ANTI-NIKE BOYCOTT...

WHICH IS FINE, THOUGH I HAVE TO ADMIT I DIDN'T EXPECT HER TO GET SO INTO IT.

WHAT ARE YOU WEARING ON YOUR FEET?

HEY, C'MON, BABE, I TAPED OVER THE SWOOSH...

KIM, WE NEED TO TALK ABOUT PRODUCT...

NO KIDDING.

I KNOW, AND I'VE GOT IT COVERED.

YOU DO?

OUR DEBUT PRODUCT WILL BE A PROPRIETARY DATABASE OF NIKE LABOR ABUSES!

I SEE A WEB PRESENCE AND A CD-ROM OF STATS, WORKER AFFIDAVITS, HUMAN RIGHTS REPORTS AND HIDDEN CAMERA VIDEO-CLIPS!

THIS IS OUR DEBUT?

KIND OF A NICHE PRODUCT, ISN'T IT, BABE?

NO. THIS WILL BE BIG— HUGE!

UM... KIM, CAN WE TALK ABOUT THIS? I THOUGHT WE WERE DEVELOPING WEB-SITE WRITING TOOLS.

WE WERE...

BUT THAT WAS BEFORE I MET A RELATIVE EMPLOYED FOR SLAVE WAGES BY A HUGELY PROFITABLE MULTINATIONAL COMPANY!

WE HAVE A CHANCE TO ACT ON OUR PRINCIPLES HERE, MIKE, TO GET THE MESSAGE OUT, TO MAKE A DIFFERENCE!

SPEAKING OF SLAVE WAGES, MAN...

THIS ISN'T ABOUT YOU, TRENT!

ACTUALLY, IT IS. WE CAN'T BE HYPOCRITES.

LOOK, MIKE, THERE'S A REAL MARKET FOR THE TRUTH ABOUT NIKE. THE AMOUNT OF MISINFORMATION THEY PUT OUT IS AMAZING!

FOR INSTANCE, THEY BOAST THEY PAY TWICE THE $200 PER CAPITA ANNUAL INCOME IN RURAL VIETNAM. BUT THE FACTORIES ARE IN SUBURBAN SAIGON, WHERE ANNUAL INCOME APPROACHES $1,000!

THEY ALSO CLAIM THEY OFFER FREE MEDICAL CARE, ENGLISH LESSONS AND TRAINING— NONE OF IT TRUE! NIKE'S IMAGE IS HELD ALOFT BY A WEB OF DECEIT!

BUT CAN'T WE STRIP BARE THEIR LIES JUST ON WEEKENDS?

MIKE, ARE YOU SURE YOU WERE ONCE YOUNG?

YO, BABE! HOW DO YOU WANT ALL THIS NIKE STUFF ORGANIZED?

I WANT A SEPARATE PAGE FOR EACH LIE, OKAY?

YOU GOT IT, BABE.

TRENT?

MIKE-A-RINO?

I NEED YOU TO STOP CALLING MY WIFE "BABE."

NO PROBLEMO. YOU'RE THE MAN.

Row 1

Panel 1: KEN STARR, SHAKING THE GIRLFRIEND TREE.
NO... NO, I DON'T RECALL ANY TALK ABOUT FINANCES...

Panel 2: HIS INTERESTS WERE ELSE-WHERE. I REMEMBER THIS RECEPTION HE HAD ONE DAY AT THE MANSION...

Panel 3: I WAS CRAMMED INTO A DRESS I'D OUTGROWN IN HIGH SCHOOL. BILL LOOKED AT ME APPRE-CIATIVELY AND SAID, "SHOW ME..." HOW'D HE PUT IT?

Panel 4: THE MONEY! SHOW ME THE **MONEY!**
DON'T BE SILLY. HE WASN'T **THAT** BIG A DEAL!

Row 2

Panel 1: DEBRIEFING THE BABES.
WHAT'S THIS ALL ABOUT, MR. STARR? AM I IN TROUBLE?

Panel 2: I HOPE NOT, MISS. BUT WE HAVE REASON TO BELIEVE THAT YOUR LITTLE FRIEND BILL WAS IN-VOLVED IN AN **ILLEGAL LOAN!**
>GASP!< **WHAT?**

Panel 3: OH, MR. STARR! I HAD NO **IDEA** BILL WAS MIXED UP IN ANY FUNNY BUSINESS! HON-EST TO GOD! I HAD NO IDEA!

Panel 4: SO YOU'RE SHOCKED.
MOST DEFI-NITELY! I'D **NEVER** CHEAT WITH A MAN WHO'S DIS-HONEST!

Row 3

Panel 1: WHAT? THE TROOPER SAID I DATED THE GOVERNOR?

Panel 2: THAT'S A BIT OF A STRETCH. WHAT HAPPENED IS THAT MR. CLINTON NOTICED ME AT A RECEPTION AT THE MANSION...

Panel 3: HE SENT THE TROOPER OVER TO TELL ME HE WANTED TO DISCUSS "REAL ESTATE" WITH ME IN PRIVATE...
BINGO!

Panel 4: HE WAS JUST JOKING, OF COURSE!
DAMN...

Row 4

Panel 1: "PILLOW TALK"? WHAT, ARE YOU NUTS?

Panel 2: LET ME GET THIS STRAIGHT. YOU THINK HE BROKE THE LAW— AND THEN CONFIDED IN **ME?**

Panel 3: LIKE, ONE DAY OL' BILL JUST WHISPERED IN MY EAR, "GUESS WHAT I DID TODAY. I AR-RANGED AN **ILLEGAL LOAN!**" IS **THAT** WHAT YOU WERE HOPING?

Panel 4: UM... IT COULD HAVE HAPPENED.
DOES CON-GRESS KNOW YOU'RE THIS DESPERATE?

199

HELLO? JOANIE? IT'S LACEY. I'VE BEEN PONDERING THIS RESIGNATION BUSINESS...

I MADE UP A LITTLE LIST OF ALL OF THE PROS AND CONS. I PUT THE PROS IN ONE COLUMN, THE CONS IN ANOTHER, AND THEN I LABELED THEM SO I'D KNOW WHICH WAS WHICH.

LACEY, ARE YOU OKAY? YOU SOUND A LITTLE FUNNY...

THEN I MADE MYSELF A PERFECTLY LOVELY CUP OF TEA.

I'M COMING OVER FOR A TALK, OKAY?

COULD YOU, DEAR? WE'LL LOOK FOR THE LIST TOGETHER.

YOU NEEDN'T HAVE DROPPED BY, DEAR. I'M SURE MY LIST WILL SHOW UP...

I KNOW YOU THINK IT'S FURTHER EVIDENCE OF MY IMPAIRMENT, BUT I'VE ALWAYS BEEN FORGETFUL. THAT'S WHY MY FILOFAX IS POSITIVELY BULGING!

YOU KEEP A FILOFAX?

I'VE HAD ONE FOR YEARS!

SEEN IT LATELY?

I DON'T REALLY NEED IT, DEAR. I HAVE A SECRETARY.

200

I'M SORRY, DEAR, I SIMPLY CAN'T RESIGN! ESPECIALLY WITH MY DREAM OF A BALANCED BUDGET BY 2000 UNFULFILLED!

BUT YOU **HAVE** FULFILLED IT, LACEY—THE BUDGET WAS PASSED TWO WEEKS AGO!

WHAT? ARE YOU SURE? WAS IT WRITTEN UP?

IT WAS INDEED. EVERYONE'S BEEN CALLING IT HISTORIC!

GRACIOUS! SO **THAT'S** WHY I'VE BEEN FEELING SO GIDDY AND GIRLISH LATELY!

MUST BE.

A MYSTERY SOLVED! ALL THE DOCTORS WERE COMPLETELY STUMPED!

I CAN'T BELIEVE WE BALANCED THE BUDGET, DEAR. I WASN'T SURE I'D LIVE TO SEE IT!

THAT'S WHAT'S MAGICAL ABOUT THIS PLACE. DESPITE ALL OUR PETTY DIFFERENCES, EVERY NOW AND THEN WE GET TOGETHER AND MAKE HISTORY HAPPEN.

THERE ARE SO MANY THINGS I'D MISS IF I WERE TO LEAVE...

LIKE WHAT?

CONGRESSWOMAN? THE PRESIDENT ON LINE TWO!

WELL, LIKE THAT. I STILL GET GOOSE BUMPS.

...AND AS A RESULT OF MY IMPAIRED MENTAL CAPABILITIES, I MUST REGRETFULLY RESIGN MY HOUSE SEAT.

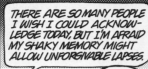

THERE ARE SO MANY PEOPLE I WISH I COULD ACKNOWLEDGE TODAY, BUT I'M AFRAID MY SHAKY MEMORY MIGHT ALLOW UNFORGIVABLE LAPSES.

THAT BEING THE CASE, I THOUGHT I'D TALK BRIEFLY ABOUT SOMETHING I'M STILL VERY MUCH IN COMMAND OF...

MY PRINCIPLES.

UH-OH...

AS YOU ALL KNOW, I HAVE MANY SHORTCOMINGS, BUT ONE OF THEM IS NOT CYNICISM. I STILL BELIEVE IN THE POSSIBILITY OF PRUDENT, RESPONSIBLE GOVERN-/MENT!

GOVERNMENT *CAN* MAKE A DIFFERENCE IN PEOPLE'S LIVES. BUT ONLY IF THOSE OF US IN PUBLIC SERVICE CONDUCT OURSELVES WITH HONOR, DIGNITY AND HUMILITY!

OF COURSE, ONE OF THE FEW ADVANTAGES OF MY AFFLICTION IS THAT I HAVE NO CLEAR IDEA OF HOW WELL I'VE MEASURED UP TO MY OWN STANDARDS!

OH, DEAR... DID THAT SOUND LIKE I WAS FISHING?

WELL, THERE'S THE HUMILITY.

THERE ARE, OF COURSE, A FEW THINGS I WON'T MISS — VICIOUS SMEAR ATTACKS IN PLACE OF CIVIL DISCOURSE...

THE SLAVISH DEPENDENCE ON OPINION POLLS TO SHAPE POLICIES ONCE BUILT ON PRINCIPLE...

THE UTTER LACK OF COMMON DECENCY IN PURSUING THE PUBLIC'S RIGHT TO KNOW...

WHAT'S SHE TALKING ABOUT?

IT'LL COME TO YOU.

WELL, I SUPPOSE THAT'S ALL I REALLY WANTED TO SAY TODAY...

I'D BE HAPPY TO TAKE ANY QUESTIONS NOW IF...

MRS. DAVENPORT, IS YOUR RESIGNATION EFFECTIVE IMMEDIATELY?

YES, IT IS, MR..... MR....

HEDLEY! ROLAND BURTON HEDLEY, JR! ABC NEWS? TWO EMMYS? HELLO?

MR. HEDLEY, YES...

POOR WOMAN — SHE REALLY *IS* FAR GONE!

POPPY, WHO'S THE OLD GUY IN THE GARAGE USING MY MAC?

THAT'S LARS, HONEY. KIM HIRED HIM TO BE OUR COMPANY VISIONARY.

WHAT'S A VISIONARY?

HE'S SOMEONE WHO TRIES TO IMAGINE WHERE THE INDUSTRY IS GOING. WE PAY HIM TO THINK ABOUT OUR COMPANY'S FUTURE.

OH.

WELL, AT THE MOMENT YOU'RE PAYING HIM TO PLAY SOLITAIRE.

VISIONARIES ARE ALLOWED TO DO THAT, SWEETHEART.

LARS? GOT A MOMENT?

SURE, IF YOU DON'T MIND SHATTERING MY CONCENTRATION.

SORRY. I WAS JUST WONDERING WHEN YOU, AS HOUSE VISIONARY, ENVISIONED SENDING ME YOUR FIRST MEMO.

HOW ABOUT WHEN IT'S READY?

...UNLESS YOU WANT ME TO SPIN YOU SOME DAZZLING, FACILE, FUTURISTIC SCENARIO JUST TO ASSURE YOU I'M AS BRILLIANT AS EVERYONE SAYS I AM!

UM..., THAT WOULD BE GOOD...

OH, PLEASE, YOU DON'T PAY ME ENOUGH!

LARS, I DON'T MEAN TO PRESSURE YOU. I JUST WANT TO KNOW...

EXCUSE ME, BUT I'M NOT MAKING DELI SANDWICHES HERE, OKAY?

CREATING THE PARADIGMS FOR THE NEXT MILLENNIUM ISN'T SOMETHING YOU CAN JUST ORDER UP! IT'S A PROCESS — IT CAN TAKE DAYS OR MONTHS OR YEARS! OKAY?

BLACK QUEEN ON RED KING.

I KNOW, I KNOW! DO YOU MIND?

KIM, WHAT'S THE STORY ON LARS? HE HASN'T PRODUCED A THING SINCE HE ARRIVED!

PATIENCE, MIKE — IMAGINING THE FUTURE AIN'T EASY...

YEAH, ESPECIALLY OURS. WHERE'D YOU FIND THIS GUY, ANYWAY?

M.I.T. MEDIA LAB. LARS WAS ONE OF MY ADVISERS.

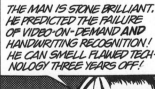

THE MAN IS STONE BRILLIANT. HE PREDICTED THE FAILURE OF VIDEO-ON-DEMAND AND HANDWRITING RECOGNITION! HE CAN SMELL FLAWED TECHNOLOGY THREE YEARS OFF!

HE ONLY PREDICTS FAILURE?

ONLY? DOES A SEISMOLOGIST ONLY PREDICT EARTHQUAKES?

204

205

206

MADAME TRIAGE? IT'S BARBARA ANN BOOP-STEIN! I NEED AN EMERGENCY HORO-SCOPE!

CERTAINLY, DARLING GIRL...

YOU ARE FACED WITH A GREAT OPPORTUNITY IN YOUR LIFE—A MINI-SERIES, PERHAPS. YOU'RE CONCERNED THAT YOUR HUSBAND WILL LEAVE YOU BEFORE THE FIRST HIATUS.

NO, ACTUALLY MY CAREER'S IN THE TOILET, AND MY HUSBAND JUST GOT A COACHING OFFER THAT WOULD TAKE US BACK TO NEW ENGLAND.

THAT'S WHAT I MEANT.

WOW... THAT'S AMAZING. ARE YOU SURE YOU CHARGE ENOUGH?

I'M SORRY, B.D., BUT I DON'T **WANT** TO MOVE! MY MALIBU LIFE IS MY ALL-TIME FAVORITE!

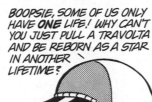

BOOPSIE, SOME OF US ONLY HAVE **ONE** LIFE! WHY CAN'T YOU JUST PULL A TRAVOLTA AND BE REBORN AS A STAR IN ANOTHER LIFETIME?

YOU'VE REALLY THOUGHT THIS THROUGH, HAVEN'T YOU?

UM... YEAH. SEEMED ONLY FAIR.

207

PRESIDENT KING? SID KIBBITZ HERE! I REP YOUR NEW PROSPECT, B.D.!

LISTEN, KINGMEISTER, I DON'T WANNA BUST YOUR STONES HERE, BUT I'M GONNA NEED A 5-YEAR PACKAGE WITH A 200 G BASE, AND A GROSS POSITION ON THE GATE!

SO TALK TO ME, CUPCAKE! KEEP ME INTERESTED! KEEP ME ON THE LINE.

HA, HA, HA, HA, HA, HA!

UH... IS THERE A PROBLEM HERE?

I'M SORRY—IT'S JUST YOU SOUND LIKE SOME RIDICULOUS HOLLYWOOD AGENT.

YOU GOT A DEAL? ALREADY?

PACK YOUR BAGS, BABE — I PROMISED YOU THERE YESTERDAY!

WHAT ARE THE TERMS?

WELL, I ASKED FOR A 5-YEAR PACKAGE WITH A 200 G BASE PLUS POINTS...

HE WOULDN'T GO FOR THE BASE OR MULTI-YEAR, BUT I DID GET YOU 85% OF THE GATE! 85%! EXCUSE ME, BUT AM I **GOOD**?

SID, THE GAMES ARE FREE.

WHOA... WHO KNEW? WELL, GOTTA RUN!

211

212

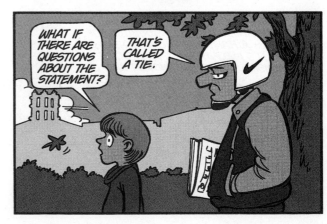

213

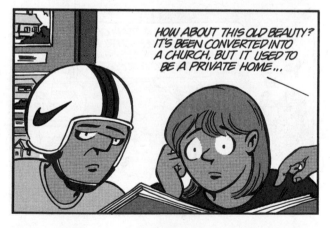

214

HERE'S SOME MORE GREAT NEWS FOR OUR LEADER, GANG...

"73% OF THE PUBLIC WOULD LIKE TO HAVE THEIR OWN INTERNS."

...AND I'M GUESSING STARR IS A BIT SHOCKED TO LEARN JUST HOW INDULGENT WE'VE BECOME IN THIS COUNTRY.

WHILE IN THE ABSTRACT, THE PUBLIC CONDEMNS PERJURY AND OBSTRUCTION OF JUSTICE...

216

...PEOPLE SEEM ALMOST RELIEVED THAT CLINTON HASN'T COME CLEAN ABOUT HIS PRIVATE LIFE, CONSIDERING IT COUNTER-INTUITIVE TO DO OTHERWISE!

SO WILL IT COME DOWN TO AN IMPEACHMENT HEARING? THIS COMMENTATOR DOUBTS IT...

BUT IF IT DOES, YOU CAN BE SURE THAT EACH AND EVERY LEGISLATOR SITTING IN JUDGMENT OF THE PRESIDENT WILL BE GIVEN THE OPPORTUNITY TO COMMENT ON HIS OWN SEXUAL HISTORY!

LOOK, IT WAS THE '70S — EVERYBODY EXPERIMENTED WITH ADULTERY!

LET ME EXPLAIN...

THAT'S OKAY.

NEXT!

218

AND AS THE FIELDS OF FLOWERS CONTINUE TO FADE IN FRONT OF BUCKINGHAM PALACE, DECAY IS THE WATCHWORD ON THE **OTHER** SIDE OF THE GATES AS WELL!

WHITHER THE WINDSORS? INTO THE DUST BIN OF HISTORY, IF HISTORY ITSELF IS ANY GUIDE. THEIR ONLY POSSIBLE SALVATION LIES IN LEARNING TO "GET IT" ABOUT THE LIVES OF ORDINARY BRITONS.

SOURCES SAY THE QUEEN WILL SHORTLY BE SEEKING THE ADVICE OF ONE OF HER OWN—A FELLOW ARISTOCRAT MORE IN TUNE WITH THE WAYS OF COMMON FOLK!

MAY WE SPEAK WITH LORD ZONKER, PLEASE?

THIS IS HIM. HE. WHOMEVER.

YES, IS THIS VISCOUNT ST. AUSTELL-IN-THE-MOOR BIGGLESWADE-BRIXHAM?

I GUESS. I CAN NEVER REMEMBER THE WHOLE DEAL.

THIS IS LORD BUMBERSHOOT, PERSONAL SECRETARY TO HER MAJESTY! THE ROYAL FAMILY NEEDS YOU, SIR!

ME? WHY, WHAT'S UP?

WE NEED YOUR EXPERTISE AS A FORMER COMMONER! THE QUEEN HAS LOST HER COMMON TOUCH AND DOESN'T KNOW WHAT TO DO!

THE QUEEN HAS LOST HER TOUCH? THE QUEEN HAS LOST HER TOUCH?

AND SHE DOESN'T KNOW WHAT TO DO!

LORD BUMBERSHOOT, I'M SURE THE SITUATION ISN'T AS BAD AS YOU IMAGINE...

BUT THERE'S SO MUCH WE DON'T UNDERSTAND!

FOR INSTANCE, **WHY** WAS THAT GIRL SO LOVED? SHE DIDN'T EVEN HAVE A TITLE! AND WHY COULDN'T WE HAVE JUST GIVEN HER A SMALL, PRIVATE FUNERAL?

AND WHO ON **EARTH** WAS THAT PUDGY LITTLE GNOME WHO PLAYED THAT **DREADFUL** DITTY IN WESTMINSTER ABBEY?

YOU'RE RIGHT— YOU'VE GOT A PROBLEM.

ALL THAT CARRYING ON ABOUT A CANDLE!

I MUST SAY, LORD BUMBERSHOOT, IT DOES SOUND LIKE THE PALACE CROWD IS A LITTLE OUT OF TOUCH WITH THE AVERAGE NIGEL.

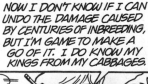

NOW I DON'T KNOW IF I CAN UNDO THE DAMAGE CAUSED BY CENTURIES OF INBREEDING, BUT I'M GAME TO MAKE A GO OF IT. I DO KNOW MY KINGS FROM MY CABBAGES.

EXCELLENT, VISCOUNT! CAN YOU LEAVE FORTHWITH?

ACTUALLY, NO. HOW ABOUT IF I COME SATURDAY?

THE MONARCHY HANGS BY A THREAD, SIR!

I KNOW, BUT I HAVE TO GET MY MARIJUANA CROP IN.

226

GOOD MORNING! ON THE EVE OF THE 21ST CENTURY, I WELCOME THE CHANCE TO HELP THE ROYAL FAMILY JOIN THE 20TH!

BY YOUR LEAVE, LET'S START WITH THE LITTLE STUFF. TAKE THE ROYAL "WE," FOR INSTANCE. ISN'T IT TIME TO STOP REFERRING TO YOURSELVES IN THE FIRST PERSON PLURAL?

CAN YOU DROP THE ROYAL "WE," YOUR HIGHNESS? CAN YOU SAY, "I, ME, MINE"?

I, ME, MINE.

BEAUTIFUL, ELIZABETH! GIVE US A HUG!

GUARD!

OKAY, FOLKS, HERE'S SUGGESTION NUMBER ONE—GET **OVER** YOURSELVES!

YOU'RE NOT RICH AND POWERFUL BECAUSE YOU'RE SPECIAL. YOU'RE RICH AND POWERFUL BECAUSE YOUR ANCESTORS STOLE WEALTH AND POWER FROM EVERYONE ELSE!

IN THE MODERN AGE, HAVING A TITLE OF **ANY** KIND IS WIDELY VIEWED AS A BADGE OF SHAME AND DISGRACE!

THEN WHY DID YOU BUY ONE?

OKAY, FAIR QUESTION. I HAVE SOME INSECURITY ISSUES.

227

OKAY, SUGGESTION NUMBER TWO— STOP MARRYING AMONG YOURSELVES!

WHEN YOU MAKE THE ARISTOCRACY A CLOSED BIO-SYSTEM, YOU'RE JUST **BEGGING** FOR TROUBLE!

IF YOU DON'T OCCASIONALLY AIR OUT YOUR GENES, YOU LOCK IN A **TOTALLY** DEBILITATING SENSE OF ENTITLEMENT!

PLUS, YOU GET YOUR IMPOTENCE AND MADNESS. YES, QUEEN MUM?

HAS ANYONE SEEN MY SLIPPERS?

...AND WELL-PLACED PALACE SOURCES CONFIRM THAT THE NEW CONSULTANT IS ONE VISCOUNT ST. AUSTELL-IN-THE-MOOR BIGGLESWADE-BRIXHAM!

THE VISCOUNT IS SAID TO HAVE BEEN REARED ABROAD IN A FREE-AND-EASY, EGALITARIAN BEACH CULTURE...

...AND THUS IS UNIQUELY QUALIFIED TO HELP THE ROYALS GET IN TOUCH WITH THEIR INNER COMMONER!

GOODBYE, ENGLAND'S ROSE...

SING OUT, MAJESTY, SING OUT!

228

WELL, B.D., IT'S GREAT TO HAVE YOU BACK!

THANK YOU, SIR...

IT'S AN HONOR TO *BE* BACK! COACHING MY OLD TEAM IS A DREAM COME TRUE FOR ME AND MY WHOLE FAMILY!

I JUST HOPE YOU'LL BE PATIENT. I'VE BEEN GOING OVER THE ROSTER, AND I'M AFRAID WE JUST DON'T HAVE THE KIND OF TALENT THAT WINS BIG GAMES.

REALLY? NOT EVEN THE GUYS WE GOT FROM PRISON?

NO, NO, THEY'RE GREAT! I'M TALKING ABOUT THE OFFENSE.

B.D., HERE'S MY PROBLEM: WE HAVE A FOOTBALL PROGRAM SO BAD WE CAN'T CHARGE FOR GAMES, AND I *NEED* THOSE REVENUES FOR MY BOTTOM LINE!

WE HAVE TO FIND A WAY TO FILL THAT STADIUM, SON!

WELL, SIR, WE MIGHT START BY SELLING BEER AND BRINGING BACK CHEERLEADERS.

BEER AND CHEERLEADERS?

IT'S THE ENTERTAINMENT TRINITY, SIR. WHAT'S VIOLENCE WITHOUT SEX AND ALCOHOL?

FRESH THINKING, SON! *FRESH* THINKING!

THANKS. I'VE BEEN LIVING IN L.A.

WELL, B.D., HERE'S YOUR CONTRACT. LOOK IT OVER, SIGN IT, GET IT BACK TO US, AND WE'RE IN BUSINESS!

B.D., I'M SURE I DON'T HAVE TO TELL YOU HOW IMPORTANT IT IS TO GET THE FOOTBALL TEAM BACK ON TRACK...

WE DON'T EXPECT YOU TO WIN THE FIRST TIME OUT, OF COURSE. BUT AS YOUR CONTRACT SUGGESTS, WE DO EXPECT YOU TO GROW IN THE JOB OVER TIME!

BUT IT'S... IT'S ONLY FOR SIX GAMES.

I DIDN'T INVENT THE '90s, SON.

I'M SORRY WE CAN'T OFFER YOU A LONGER CONTRACT, B.D., BUT WE'RE LIVING IN A VERY RESULTS-DRIVEN CULTURE NOW...

THERE'S JUST TOO MUCH REVENUE AT STAKE, AS A SPORTS PROFESSIONAL, YOU SURELY UNDERSTAND.

YES, AND DON'T WORRY, SIR— I'LL GET THIS TEAM WINNING AGAIN!

GOOD. NOW HERE'S YOUR PLAYBOOK. IT WAS PROVIDED BY OUR SPONSOR...

SPONSOR?

JUST SO YOU KNOW— THEY LIKE THE PASSING GAME.

OKAY, GUYS, **GOOD** PRACTICE! I LIKED WHAT I SAW OUT THERE TODAY!

THIS TEAM HAS **DEFINITELY** GOT THE TALENT TO TURN THINGS AROUND, TO START WINNING FOOTBALL GAMES AGAIN!

IF WE WORK HARD, WE CAN MAKE THAT HAPPEN! WE **WILL** MAKE IT HAPPEN! ANY QUESTIONS?

COACH?

YEAH?

WHEN DO WE GET OUR TATTOOS?

YOU SHOWED GOOD HUSTLE TODAY, SOKOL!

HEY THANKS, COACH...

IT'S A REAL HONOR TO BE PLAYING FOR SOME-ONE WHO'S BEEN THERE, KNOW WHAT I'M SAYIN'?

I'VE BEEN READIN' IN THE CAMPUS RAG ABOUT THE TEAMS YOU PLAYED ON! YOU GUYS **ROCKED**, MAN! IT MUSTA BEEN A **KILLER** RUSH FOR YOU, RIGHT?

WELL, YES, I SUPPOSE IT...

I MEAN, TO PLAY WITH A LEGEND LIKE ZONKER HARRIS! **FORGET** ABOUT IT!

229

YOU'RE OFF TO WHAT, BABE?

MY 20TH REUNION. AT BOALT HALL...

UM...IS THIS SOME-THING WE DISCUSSED?

OH, COME ON, RICK— AGES AGO!

WHY DID YOU THINK I WAS EXERCISING AND DIETING LIKE A MADWOMAN DURING THE PAST FEW MONTHS?

UM... FOR ME.

OH, PLEASE. I'LL CALL.

MAY I GET YOU A DRINK, MA'AM?

YES, WHITE WINE, PLEASE.

JOAN GIRL!

UH-OH...

JOAN, IT'S **ME**, WOODY! HOW YOU **BEEN**?

WELL, FINE, WOODY, I...

INCREDIBLE! WOULD YOU BELIEVE I RE-MEMBER YOU AS A TOTAL **TUBBO**? IS THAT A RIOT?

YES, THAT WOULD BE A RIOT, WOODY.

I MEAN, WOW! YOU WITH SOME-ONE, OR CAN I HIT ON YOU?

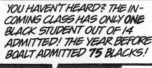

230

I CAN SEE WHY YOU'D BE A LITTLE UNSETTLED BY THIS CLYDE FELLOW, MRS. D— I'VE BEEN IN THE **SAME** POSITION!

MY NEMESIS, THADEUS MORANE, TOOK OVER THE MARYLAND AUDUBON SOCIETY NEWSLETTER FROM ME! ALL BECAUSE OF A FEW TYPOS! WHICH **I** DIDN'T MAKE!

THERE WAS FUNNY BUSINESS! I'M **SURE** OF IT!

DEAR, WHICH OF US IS DEMENTED? I CAN NEVER REMEMBER.

DEAR, WHAT'S THAT WHITE MARBLE SPIRE CALLED? I'VE FORGOTTEN...

YOU MEAN, THE WASHINGTON MONUMENT?

YES, THE WASHINGTON MONUMENT. I NEVER NOTICED WHAT AN ODD-LOOKING STRUCTURE IT IS!

IT'S REALLY DREADFULLY PHALLIC, ISN'T IT?

LACEY! WE DON'T USE WORDS LIKE THAT! ESPECIALLY YOU!

ALL RIGHT, THEN, IT'S PHALLIC AS HELL.

I BETTER CALL YOUR DOCTOR.

232

...AND SHE'S STARTING TO USE THIS INCREDIBLY INAPPROPRIATE LANGUAGE, DOCTOR!

WELL, THAT'S GOING TO HAPPEN, JEREMY...

I'M SURE THE BEHAVIORAL CHANGES ARE UPSETTING, BUT IT'S IMPORTANT TO STAY COOL AND FOCUS ON THE BIG STUFF— LIKE WANDERING.

WANDERING?

YES. WHERE IS LACEY NOW?

HELLO? MAY I JOIN YOU?

PROBABLY. LET ME CHECK MY DATE BOOK, SUGAR.

IT'S LOVELY TO SEE YOU AGAIN, PEARL!

SAME BACK ATCHA, PRINCESS. ONLY MY NAME AIN'T PEARL— IT'S ALICE.

NONSENSE, PEARL. YOU DON'T THINK I KNOW MY OWN SISTER'S NAME?

YOU DON'T THINK I KNOW MY **OWN** NAME? IT'S ALICE, I TELL YOU!

OKAY, OKAY...

DON'T TELL MOTHER YOU CHANGED IT. IT'D KILL HER.

OKAY. AM I GETTING ANYTHING, BY THE WAY?

Panel 1: WERE YOU SHOCKED TO FIND OUT WHO THE BUYERS WERE, SCOT? / A LITTLE—BUT MOSTLY I WAS VERY, VERY PLEASED.

Panel 2: I HATE TO LEAVE, BUT MY MINISTRY HAS OUTGROWN WALDEN. IT'S OF GREAT COMFORT TO KNOW THE PLACE IS GOING TO YOU!

Panel 3: AS YOU KNOW, IT'S QUITE A SPECIAL HOUSE. COME ON IN AND GET RE-ACQUAINTED!

Panel 4: MY... YOU CERTAINLY KEEP IT COOL, SCOT. / NO, THE BOILER'S JUST SHOT. I'LL MAKE A FIRE.

Panel 5: AS YOU CAN SEE, THERE'VE BEEN SEVERAL ADDITIONS TO WALDEN SINCE YOU LIVED HERE. I'M SURE IT'S ALMOST UNRECOGNIZABLE...

Panel 6: THE SECOND FLOOR WE CONVERTED TO MEETING ROOMS— MOSTLY FOR TAI-CHI AND 12-STEP.

Panel 7: AND THIS ROOM WE'VE BEEN USING AS A CHAPEL... / MY OLD BEDROOM IS A CHAPEL? HOW FITTING.

Panel 8: FITTING? / YEAH—IT'S WHERE MY PRAYERS WERE FIRST ANSWERED. TWICE. / B.D.!

Panel 9: SCOT, I CAN'T *TELL* YOU HOW EXCITED WE ARE TO BE MOVING BACK INTO THIS GREAT OLD HOUSE!

Panel 10: IT'S JUST SUCH A WONDERFUL ENVIRONMENT FOR SAM TO GROW UP IN...

Panel 11: ESPECIALLY THE NATURAL SURROUNDINGS. I CAN'T WAIT FOR HER TO SEE ZONKER'S BELOVED POND!

Panel 12: WE LEFT MALIBU FOR THIS? / IT SEEMED BIGGER.

Panel 13: SO THIS IS SORT OF WHERE I CAME OF AGE, SAM, WHERE I MADE KEY LIFESTYLE CHOICES!

Panel 14: I THINK IT'S SAFE TO SAY I NEVER LOOKED BACK! / ZONK, WERE YOU A HIPPIE?

Panel 15: WAS I A HIPPIE? HA, HA! WELL, I... I...

Panel 16: I DON'T RECALL. / YOU WERE A HIPPIE.

ZONKER, HOW COME YOU HAD TO STAY IN ENGLAND SO LONG?

WELL, SAM, IT TOOK A WHILE TO PUT THE ROYALS IN TOUCH WITH THEIR INNER COMMONERS...

AND THEN, JUST AS I WAS GETTING READY TO LEAVE, CHAS CALLED ME IN TO DEFEND THE AU PAIR VERDICT!

I MEAN, I HAD **163** NANNIES, AND NOT **ONE** OF THEM TRIED TO KILL ME!

GOOD POINT, SIR.

WASHINGTON, D.C.—WHERE FOR ALL ITS POMP AND CIRCUMSTANCE...

...ITS PHYSICAL GRANDEUR AND GLORY, ITS LOVE OF PAGEANTRY AND OCCASION...

...THERE ARE STILL FEW THINGS **HALF** AS EXCITING...

...AS THE ARRIVAL OF A NEW LAWMAKER.

AND I'LL BE TELLING THE PRESIDENT TO STUFF IT!

CLYDE ARRIVES ON THE HILL.

GOOD MORNING, LADIES AND GENTLEMEN. I'M CONGRESSMAN CLYDE MONTANA...

AND I NOW REPRESENT LACEY DAVENPORT'S OLD DISTRICT. SOME OF YOU MAY HAVE BEEN TRACKING MY METEORIC CAREER FROM AFAR...

...SINCE I FIRST BURST INTO NATIONAL PROMINENCE AS A LEADING ARCHITECT OF CALIFORNIA'S PROPOSITION 209 BANNING AFFIRMATIVE ACTION!

EASILY THE MOST DISGRACEFUL THING HE'S EVER DONE.!

AND THIS IS MY LOVELY WIFE GINNY.

AND I HOPE TO BRING TO THE JOB THE SAME KIND OF FRESH THINKING I BROUGHT TO THE EFFORT TO PASS PROP 209 IN CALIFORNIA...

WHICH, AS YOU KNOW, HAS BEEN A HUGE SUCCESS!

WHAT?

BUT HAVEN'T MINORITY ADMISSIONS FALLEN BADLY?

YES, BUT LIKE A BADLY OVERVALUED STOCK, THEY NEEDED TO. MOST OF THE KIDS WHO USED TO BE ACCEPTED WEREN'T UP TO ADVANCED EDUCATION.

WELL, NOW, THAT'S JUST A **LIE**, CLYDE!

MS. SLADE, PLEASE—LET US DO OUR JOB!

SO, YES, I GUESS I DO LOOK AT AFFIRMATIVE ACTION SOMEWHAT DIFFERENTLY THAN MY HUSBAND...

YOU HAVE TO ASK YOURSELVES, WHAT WOULD AMERICA BE LIKE TODAY *WITHOUT* THESE POLICIES OF INCLUSION? WOULD THERE EVEN *BE* A BLACK MIDDLE CLASS?

CONGRESSMAN, YOU AND YOUR WIFE SEEM TO HAVE LITTLE IN COMMON POLITICALLY. WHAT'S BEEN THE SECRET TO THE LONGEVITY OF YOUR MARRIAGE?

HEE, HEE! WELL, AS A PUBLIC OFFICIAL, I'M RELUCTANT TO DISCUSS SEX...

UNDERSTANDABLY!

LADIES AND GENTLEMEN, I KNOW I DON'T CONFORM TO YOUR LIMITED NOTIONS OF WHAT A BLACK REPRESENTATIVE SHOULD BE...

BUT THAT'S YOUR PROBLEM, NOT MINE! I CAME HERE TO SHAKE UP THOSE OLD MODELS OF DEPENDENCY AND DESPAIR—AND REPLACE THEM WITH OPPORTUNITY AND HOPE!

IN THAT SENSE, YOU COULD SAY I'M PART OF A NEW BREED!

CONGRESSMAN, WHAT'S YOUR FIRST ORDER OF BUSINESS?

UM... RAISING MONEY.

WE'RE ALREADY LATE FOR OUR FIRST EVENT.

236

WELL, I THINK THAT WENT PRETTY WELL, DON'T YOU?

CLYDE, LET ME ASK YOU SOMETHING...

IN THIS GOLDEN ERA BACK BEFORE AFFIRMATIVE ACTION, WHEN MINORITY STUDENTS WERE ADMITTED STRICTLY ON MERIT AND THE "CONTENT OF THEIR CHARACTERS"...

DO YOU RECALL WHAT THOSE STUDENTS WERE CALLED?

UM... TOKENS, BUT...

BRIMMING WITH SELF-ESTEEM, WERE THEY?

MAN, WHAT A TURNOUT! ISN'T IT AMAZING WHAT A WINNING SEASON CAN DO?

B.D., I'M *SO* NERVOUS!

NERVOUS? ABOUT WHAT?

B.D., I DON'T KNOW ANYONE HERE YET. I WANT TO MAKE A GOOD IMPRESSION AT THE COLLEGE, BE TAKEN SERIOUSLY!

RELAX, IT'S JUST A FOOTBALL BANQUET. LOOK, THERE'S SOME GUYS FROM THE TEAM—WAVE!

NO *WAY* SHE DID FULL FRONTAL IN "PORKY'S"!

WAY, DUDE. I OWN THE TAPE, OKAY?

AND AFTER LUNCH, I THOUGHT WE'D DECORATE THE TREE! DOES THAT SOUND LIKE FUN, ALEX?

NO, IT SOUNDS BORING.

NOW, DON'T BE LIKE THAT, SWEETHEART...

WE'VE ONLY GOT FIVE DAYS TOGETHER, BUT IT CAN BE A WONDERFUL HOLIDAY, FULL OF ALL THE SPECIAL THINGS ABOUT CHRISTMAS THAT YOU'VE ALWAYS LOVED!

YEAH, LIKE, KIDNAPPING IS **SO** CHRISTMASY.

IT'S CALLED CUSTODY. JOINT CUSTODY.

ISN'T THIS FUN, HONEY? IT'S BEEN SO LONG SINCE WE'VE DONE TRADITIONAL CHRISTMAS STUFF!

UH-HUH...

DONG!

HEY, DID I JUST HEAR THE DOORBELL! I BELIEVE I DID! GO SEE WHO'S AT THE DOOR, OKAY, SWEETHEART?

I DON'T BELIEVE THIS...

HO, HO, HO! IS THERE A LITTLE GIRL HERE?

WHAT A SURPRISE! IT'S UNCLE STUPIDHEAD!

ZEKE, UNCLE ZEKE. YOU'RE PRONOUNCING IT WRONG.

238

ZEKE GOT ME A PRESENT?

YES, AND HE WENT TO A LOT OF TROUBLE!

YEAH, BUT IT WAS WORTH IT! THIS SUCKER'S GONNA BLOW YOUR LITTLE SOCKS OFF!

OH, WOW— A TICKLE-ME-ELMO! HOW THOUGHTFUL...

HEE, HEE! LIKE IT?

LAST YEAR'S HOT TOY FOR FOUR-YEAR-OLDS? WHO WOULDN'T?

DAMN STREET PEDDLERS— THEY'RE SUCH LIARS!

YOU DON'T SEEM VERY JOLLY FOR CHRISTMAS MORNING, MIKE...

I KNOW... I'M SORRY...

IT'S JUST THAT THIS IS THE FIRST CHRISTMAS DAY I HAVEN'T BEEN WITH ALEX SINCE SHE WAS BORN.

ALSO, LIKE EVERY OTHER DIVORCED PERSON IN THE WORLD, I'M WORRYING ABOUT HOW MY PRESENTS ARE COMPARING TO THOSE SHE'S GETTING NOW...

A CAN OF **TUNA FISH!** HEY, THANKS, UNCLE STUPIDHEAD!

IT'S THE GIFT OF PROTEIN, MAN.

240

DR. WHITAKER, IS ANYONE THINKING ABOUT CHELSEA? PEOPLE ARE SAYING SUCH MEAN THINGS ABOUT HER DAD, AND SHE'S ALL ALONE!

WELL, I CAN SEE HOW THAT MIGHT UPSET SOME OF YOU. BUT WHAT YOU HAVE TO REMEMBER IS THAT SHE HAS BEEN PREPARED FOR THIS ALL HER LIFE...

WHEN CHELSEA WAS LITTLE, HER FATHER WOULD TELL HER STORIES ABOUT HIM-SELF TO TOUGHEN HER UP.

LIKE WHAT?

WELL, LIKE, THAT HE WAS THE DEVIL.

IT MAY BE, KIDS, THAT ALL OF THIS WILL BLOW OVER...

BUT WE ALSO HAVE TO PRE-PARE OURSELVES FOR THE WORST. MR. CLINTON MIGHT WELL BE FORCED FROM OFFICE!

IF THAT HAPPENS, IF THIS TERRIBLE TRAGEDY OVER-TAKES THE PRESIDENT, DO YOU THINK WE'LL ALL BE ABLE TO COPE?

OF COURSE! AL GORE IS **JUST** AS CUTE!

AND HE'S SO STRAIGHT HE HANGS OUT WITH NUNS.

UM...EXCUSE ME, LADY WITH THE PLASTIC SHAWL?

REMEMBER ME? JEREMY CAVENDISH, LACEY'S LIVE-IN CAREGIVER? THE FELLOW WHO GAVE YOU NOT ONE BUT **TWO** DOVE BARS!

WELL, ANYWAY, I'VE SIGNED UP FOR AN ALZHEIMER'S SUPPORT GROUP, AND I NEED SOMEONE TO KEEP AN EYE ON MRS. D.! SINCE SHE SEEMS TO LIKE YOU, I THOUGHT MAYBE YOU'D GIVE IT A GO!

WELL, I...

YOU TALK TO **ME**, JUNIOR— I'M HER **AGENT**!

OKAY! WHAT DO YOU NEED? TOP DOL-LAR?

MRS. D? YOU'VE GOT A VISITOR!

SISTER DEAREST! WHAT ARE **YOU** DOING HERE?

SHE'S GOING TO KEEP YOU COMPANY WHILE I GO TO MY SUPPORT GROUP, OKAY?

SPLENDID! WE'LL HAVE SOME NICE TEA AND GET CAUGHT UP!

I'LL BE BACK IN A FEW HOURS. BE GOOD!

I SEE YOU'VE MET MARIO, MY PAPER BOY.

YUP. WOULD YOU HAVE A DRUMSTICK OR SOMETHING TO GO WITH THIS?

TONIGHT I'D LIKE TO WELCOME MR. JEREMY CAVENDISH TO OUR SUPPORT GROUP...

JEREMY, EVERYONE HERE IS ENDURING THE WRENCHING EXPERIENCE OF WATCHING A LOVED ONE SLIP AWAY FROM US...

IT'S AN ORDEAL THAT OFTEN ISOLATES. MOST PRIMARY CAREGIVERS FEEL TERRIBLY ALONE MUCH OF THE TIME...

NOT ME!

UH... YOU DON'T?

NOPE! I JUST TALK TO MYSELF! AT A PRETTY HEALTHY CLIP, TOO!

AND THE REASON I SOUGHT OUT THIS ALZHEIMER'S SUPPORT GROUP IS THAT I'M GOING CRAZY WITH MRS. D!

SOME DAYS SHE THINKS I'M HER SUITOR, SOME DAYS I'M HER NURSE, SOME DAYS HER PAPER BOY! I GET **SO** CONFUSED! I NEVER KNOW WHAT TO **WEAR**!

I'VE GOT A HOUSECOAT THAT GIVES ME SOME FLEXIBILITY, BUT IT ISN'T ME! I BOUGHT IT IN MARRAKECH IN '73, BUT THE LIGHT WAS BAD! WHAT TO DO! I'M AT **WIT'S END**, I TELL YOU!

AND YOU'RE QUITE SURE **YOU'RE** NOT THE PATIENT, HON?

POSITIVE! I CAN DOUBLE-CHECK, BUT IT WOULDN'T DO ANY GOOD!

247

OKAY, THIS IS WHAT HAPPENS ALL THE TIME! ALL THE TIME! MRS. D DOES SOMETHING THAT IRRITATES ME! THEN SHE DOES IT **AGAIN**!

THAT MAKES ME ANGRY, WHICH SENDS ME INTO A SHAME SPIRAL, BECAUSE IT'S NOT HER FAULT! FINALLY, I SINK INTO DESPAIR!

WELL, JEREMY, YOU...

TO SUM UP, THEN: IRRITATION, ANGER, SHAME AND DESPAIR!

I THINK WE GET THE PICTURE, HON.

GOOD DEAL! ANY TIPS? I'M RUNNING LATE!

I GUESS WHAT IT COMES DOWN TO IS I **MISS** BEING ALL THE THINGS I WAS BEFORE I MADE MY COMMITMENT TO MRS. D'S CARE!

I MISS JEREMY THE RAKE, JEREMY THE RACONTEUR, JEREMY THE GADABOUT! THOSE JEREMYS TAKE A BACKSEAT WHEN YOU'RE ATTENDING TO A LOVED ONE AROUND THE CLOCK!

UH... WHO'S WITH HER NOW?

NOT TO WORRY— I LEFT HER WITH A TRUSTED HOMELESS PERSON.

I'VE GOT AN IDEA, DUCKS— LET'S TRADE PLACES!

WHAT FUN!

WHY, HELLO, DEAR HEART!

HUH?

AREN'T YOU REGGIE, MY SISTER PEARL'S SECOND HUSBAND?

DEPENDS! WHO'S ASKIN'?

IT'S LACEY, YOUR SISTER-IN-LAW! PEARL AND I ARE SWITCHING PLACES FOR THE DAY! AS A LARK! AREN'T WE JUST WICKED?

AND YOUR PEOPLE ARE OKAY WITH THIS? I DOUBT IT, LADY!

YOU KNOW, MRS. D, THERE'S SOMETHING DIFFERENT ABOUT YOU...

IT'LL COME TO YOU.

YOU WHAT?

WE TRADED PLACES. AS A LARK. DON'T WORRY—IT'S JUST FOR THE DAY...

GOOD GOD, WOMAN—WHERE IS SHE?

IN THE PARK. SHE'S SAFE AS PIE. ELMONT WILL KEEP AN EYE ON HER.

BUT THIS IS OUTRAGEOUS! IT'S LIKE SOMETHING OUT OF DICKENS! NO, NOT DICKENS... HEMINGWAY! NO, NO, DOSTOYEVSKY!... NO...

KAFKA?

NO, NO, IT BEGINS WITH A "P"! NO, A "C"! NO, NO, A "W"!

OH, YEAH, HIM.

248

YOU LET LACEY GO SIT IN THE PARK WITH ELMONT? ARE YOU OUT OF YOUR MIND?

WELL, IT'S ALL RELATIVE, DUCKS...

I MEAN, LET'S LOOK AT THE PLAYERS. LACEY IS SUFFERING FROM DEMENTIA, ELMONT'S SCHIZOPHRENIC AND YOU'RE CLINICALLY DYSFUNCTIONAL...

FROM WHERE I'M SITTING, I'M THE ONLY ONE OF OUR LITTLE GANG STILL IN POSSESSION OF ALL HER MARBLES.

GOOD GOD, YOU'RE RIGHT! YOU'RE OUR ONLY HOPE!

EXACTLY. WHICH IS WHY I HAVE TO KEEP MY STRENGTH UP.

SEE, PEARL HAD ALWAYS WONDERED ABOUT MY GRACIOUS LIFESTYLE, AND I'D ALWAYS BEEN CURIOUS ABOUT HERS!

UH-HUH...

SO WE AGREED—SHE WOULD PLAY TOWNHOUSE MOUSE FOR THE DAY, AND I WOULD GIVE THE OUTDOORSY LIFE A WHIRL! I MUST SAY, SO FAR I LOVE IT!

AHEM... AHEM?

WHAT? WHAT IS IT NOW?

I CAN'T SEEM TO CATCH THE TOWEL BOY'S EYE...

HE'S MARRIED. DON'T GO THERE.

ISN'T IT JUST THE MOST GLORIOUS DAY, REGGIE? ISN'T IT JUST THE GRANDEST?

DO YOU **MIND?** I'M TRYING TO GET THE SKINNY ON THE EMBATTLED YEN!

OH... SORRY, DEAR.

LET'S DO SOMETHING GAY, REG! LET'S GO SAILING!

NO CAN DO. MY ANKLE BRACELET WOULD SHORT OUT.

WELL, I BETTER BE GOING. MY HOUSEBOY WILL WORRY...

REG, BE A DEAR AND TELL ME HOW TO GET HOME. MY ADDRESS IS ON MY BRACELET...

3058 "M" STREET, HUH?

THAT'S EASY! TAKE THREE RIGHTS AND A LEFT, GO UP TWO FLIGHTS, HOP OVER THE CHAIN-LINK FENCE, AND HIGHTAIL IT ACROSS THE RAIL YARDS...

I'M NOT ASKING THE RIGHT PERSON, AM I?

WHEN YOU GET TO THE RIVER, LASH TOGETHER SOME TIRES...

DOOR, SOMEBODY!

I GOT IT!...

MAY I HELP YOU?

RICHARD REDFERN?

YES?

RICHARD REDFERN WHO AS A REPORTER WITTINGLY PARTICIPATED IN A CONCERTED WHITE HOUSE EFFORT TO MAKE THE INDEPENDENT COUNSEL'S OFFICE LOOK BAD?

IF YOU SAY SO, WHAT'S UP?

YOUR SUBPOENA.

GET OUT! STARR **SUBPOENAED** YOU?

I'M DUE TO APPEAR TOMORROW...

WHY ON EARTH WOULD HE WANT TO SUBPOENA A REPORTER?

WELL, HE'S QUITE CLEAR ABOUT THAT...

"TO ANSWER QUESTIONS AS TO WHETHER YOU WILLFULLY AND WANTONLY ABETTED A WHITE HOUSE CONSPIRACY TO HURT THE FEELINGS OF THE HONORABLE KENNETH W. STARR."

OH, DEAR...

AS YOU CAN IMAGINE, I'M JUST SICK ABOUT THIS.

RICK! DO YOU KNOW WHY YOU'RE BEING HAULED INTO THE STARR CHAMBER?

NO, BUT I'M VERY PROUD TO HAVE BEEN CHOSEN. BEING SUBPOENAED BY STARR IS LIKE MAKING NIXON'S ENEMIES LIST— IT HAS A CERTAIN CACHET...

AFTER ALL, IT'S ONLY THE REAL PLAYERS WHO SEEM TO BE GETTING SUBPOENAS, RIGHT, ROLAND?

UH... RIGHT!

I ASSUME YOU GOT ONE, TOO?

UH... NO. I'VE BEEN ON THE ROAD. WHO SHOULD I CALL?

MR. REDFERN, AS A REPORTER, HAVE YOU EVER RECEIVED INFORMATION UNFLATTERING TO MR. STARR'S OFFICE?

YES, I HAVE.

AND WOULD YOU TELL THE GRAND JURY WHAT THAT INFORMATION WAS EXACTLY?

I'D BE HAPPY TO, MR. UDOLF.

MY SOURCES INFORMED ME OF PAST MISCONDUCT ON THE PART OF STARR'S TOP AIDES. I WAS TOLD THAT YOU YOURSELF WERE ONCE FOUND GUILTY OF VIOLATING A DEFENDANT'S CIVIL RIGHTS.

AND YOU PRINTED THIS TRASH TALK?

WE FIGURED REAL COWBOYS COULD HANDLE IT. WHO KNEW?

250

MR. REDFERN, WHAT DID YOUR WHITE HOUSE SOURCE SAY ABOUT MR. STARR SPECIFICALLY?

HE SAID LOTS OF MEAN THINGS. I REPORTED THEM ALL.

AND YOU AND YOUR SOURCE WEREN'T AT ALL CONCERNED THAT SUCH CRITICISM MIGHT BE ILLEGAL?

NOPE. WE WERE BOTH UNDER THE IMPRESSION THAT THE SEDITION ACT EXPIRED NEARLY 200 YEARS AGO.

UH... IT DID?

CAN'T YOU GUYS AFFORD LAW CLERKS?

OKAY, I KNOW YOU'RE ALL DYING TO KNOW WHO I GAVE UP TODAY...

AS EXPECTED, I WAS GRILLED ON MY WHITE HOUSE SOURCE AND ASKED TO DETAIL HIS CRITICISMS OF THE INDEPENDENT COUNSEL'S OFFICE.

I REPLIED THAT I HAD OVER 20 SOURCES, AND THAT THEY HAD DESCRIBED MR. STARR VARIOUSLY AS PARTISAN, UNETHICAL, DISHONEST, CORRUPT, EGOMANIACAL, GREEDY, BLAND AND OUT OF CONTROL.

AND YOU REPORTED ALL THIS?

YEAH. EXCEPT BLAND. I COULDN'T CONFIRM BLAND.

ZONKER, HOW COME THE PRESIDENT'S IN SO MUCH TROUBLE LATELY?

WELL, MOST LIKELY IT'S THE ECONOMY, SAM...

SEE, A LOT OF AMERICAN COMPANIES HAVE BEEN DOWNSIZING THEIR WORK FORCES, AND IT'S THROWN US INTO A MILD BUT PAINFUL RECESSION...

WITH JOBS SCARCE AND CRIME AT AN ALL-TIME HIGH, PEOPLE ARE LOOKING TO BLAME THE MAN IN CHARGE. THAT'S WHY HIS POLL NUMBERS ARE SO LOW!

©B Prudeau

WOW... WHERE DO YOU GET ALL THAT STUFF?

MY DENTIST'S WAITING ROOM. I THINK IT'S IMPORTANT TO KEEP UP.

SMELL HOW SWEET THE AIR IS, SAM? MORE THAN ANYTHING ELSE, IT'S THE SPRING AIR THAT TAKES ME BACK...

WHEN I CLOSE MY EYES, I'M THAT SAME INNOCENT SPRITE OF A LAD WHO TROD THESE GREENING MEADOWS SO MANY YEARS AGO...

...LIVING ENTIRELY IN THE PRESENT, UNBURDENED BY AMBITION OR THE SLIGHTEST NOTION OF WHERE I WAS HEADED!

©B Prudeau

WHO'D HAVE GUESSED I'D GROW UP TO BE A POWERFUL, RESPECTED BABY SITTER?

I NEED A DREAM LIKE THAT...

YIKES! ISN'T THAT COLD, ZONKER?

I'M USED TO IT, SQUIRT...

DURING MY COMMUNE DAYS, THIS WAS ONE OF MY FAVORITE SPOTS!

HOW COME?

WELL, THERE WAS AN ENERGY CRISIS ON. TO CONSERVE HEATING OIL, I'D COME DOWN HERE TO BATHE!

YOU BATHED IN POND SCUM?

UM... IT WIPES OFF.

ZONKER, DID YOU PARTY A LOT DURING YOUR COMMUNE DAYS?

YES, INDEED, LITTLE GIRL...

WE'D OFTEN STAY UP ALL NIGHT READING LINER NOTES AND STARING AT OUR FINGERS AND EXPERIMENTING WITH ALTERNATIVE LIFESTYLES!

WE DID OTHER STUFF, TOO, BUT IT'S NOT SUITABLE FOR THE EARS OF AN ALMOST-SIX-YEAR-OLD!

©B Prudeau

DID YOU GUYS HAVE AURAL SEX BACK THEN?

AURAL SEX? UH... SURE. THE WALLS WERE VERY THIN.

ZONKER, DO YOU THINK THAT ONE DAY I COULD GROW UP TO BE A HIPPIE LIKE YOU WERE?

I DON'T THINK SO, SAM. THE CONDITIONS AREN'T RIGHT. TO HAVE A COUNTERCULTURE, YOU HAVE TO HAVE INTACT INSTITUTIONS TO CHALLENGE...

UNFORTUNATELY, THERE AREN'T ANY LEFT. WHAT WE NEED IS SOMEONE WITH ENOUGH MORAL AUTHORITY TO BUILD THEM BACK UP AGAIN!

LIKE WHO?

WELL, LIKE JOE DIMAGGIO. SOMEONE LIKE THAT.

THINK HE'D TAKE THE JOB?

I CAN'T BELIEVE HOW WARM THE WATER IS ALREADY...

I GUESS WE HAVE EL NINO TO THANK FOR THIS. IT'S BEEN ONE OF THE STRANGEST WINTERS IN...

IN...

OKAY, THIS IS IMPRESSIVE.

I HOPE THE HOUSE IS OKAY.

MOMMY, I LIKE WALDEN. DO YOU THINK WE'LL LIVE HERE A LONG TIME?

WELL, HONEY, IT KIND OF DEPENDS ON WHETHER DADDY'S FOOTBALL TEAM KEEPS WINNING.

THAT'S WHY HE'S ALWAYS ON THE ROAD RECRUITING. IT'S NOT EASY TO KEEP A TEAM ON TOP YEAR AFTER YEAR.

FORTUNATELY, YOUR DADDY HAS QUITE A TALENT FOR ATTRACTING THE VERY BEST STUDENT-ATHLETES TO THE COLLEGE!

YO, I JUST NEED A PLACE TO HOTDOG 'TIL I'M DRAFTED.

YOU'RE IN LUCK, SON—WE CAN **MEET** THAT SPECIAL NEED!

PLUS, WALDEN HAS WHOLE DEPARTMENTS FULL OF PLAYER-FRIENDLY COURSES TAUGHT BY FACULTY WHO UNDERSTAND YOUR SPECIAL NEEDS.

BEFORE YOU KNOW IT, YOU'LL BE BASKING IN THE PRESTIGE OF ATTENDING A **FULLY** ACCREDITED COLLEGE—JUST LIKE THE REAL STUDENTS!

SO WHAT DO YOU THINK, SON? ANY QUESTIONS?

UH...YEAH...

WHAT'S THE DEAL WITH FOOD?

FEEDINGS ARE ON THE HOUR! PLUS, AS A STARTER, YOU GET YOUR OWN MEAT LOCKER!

COACH, I DON'T SEE ANYTHING IN HERE ABOUT PARTY PRO-TECTION.

PARTY PRO-TECTION?

YEAH, MAN, I PLAY HARD— BOTH ON THE FIELD AND OFF! WHAT IF I GET BUSTED OR I TOTAL A CAR? WHAT IF I PUNCH OUT A COP OR SOME GIRL ACCUSES ME OF DATE RAPE?

I MEAN, WOULD THE COLLEGE GET BE-HIND ME OR WHAT?

ABSOLUTELY. WE'D SET YOU UP WITH A TOP LEGAL TEAM— PLUS A PUBLICIST TO GET OUT **YOUR** SIDE OF THE STORY!

COOL. BECAUSE I GOTTA BE ME, YOU KNOW?

ABSOLUTELY. **ALL** THE GREATS HAVE HAD TO BE THEMSELVES!

COACH, I DON'T SEE IN THIS LETTER OF INTENT ANY MENTION OF AARON'S EDUCATION. WHO WILL GUIDE HIM ACADEMICALLY, MAKE SURE HE GRADUATES, GET HIM ON THE RIGHT CAREER PATH?

UH...WELL, I'D BE HAPPY TO SPELL ALL THAT OUT FOR YOU, SIR. FRANKLY, I DON'T MEET TOO MANY FATHERS INTER-ESTED IN THAT SIDE OF THE WALDEN EXPERI-ENCE!

I'M NOT HIS FA-THER.

OH...THEN YOU WOULD BE...?

I WOULD BE HIS PAROLE OFFICER.

WHATEVER, IT'S GREAT THAT YOU'RE SO INVOLVED.

HEY, COACH, BEFORE I SIGN THIS LETTER OF INTENT, I'D LIKE TO ASK YOU SOME-THING...

SHOOT, EDDIE.

COACH, I KNOW I'M GOOD, BUT I'M NOT AN IDIOT— I REALIZE A PRO CAREER ISN'T IN THE CARDS FOR ME. I'M GONNA **NEED** A COLLEGE EDUCATION!

COACH, WILL WALDEN PREPARE ME FOR THE 21st CENTURY?

EDDIE, I PERSONALLY GUARANTEE IT! WHAT DO YOU WANT TO BE?

I DUNNO— MAYBE A REPO MAN, SOMETHING LIKE THAT.

I THINK "EDDIE" HAS TWO D's.

B.D.? WHERE ARE YOU?

AT BOOMER LAPAGE'S HOUSE. HE'S IN THE OTHER ROOM CONFERRING WITH HIS AGENT.

A HIGH SCHOOL SENIOR HAS AN AGENT?

BOOPSIE, YOU WOULDN'T BE-LIEVE WHAT THESE ARRO-GANT JERKS ASK FOR!

I MEAN, THERE WERE SOME COCKY GUYS IN MY DAY, BUT THESE KIDS ARE OUT OF CON-TROL! IT'S BEEN **VERY** HARD HOLDING THE LINE HERE ...

COACH? HE WANTS A GULF-STREAM FOR AWAY GAMES.

NO PROB-LEM.

>SNIFF!<

UH-OH. SOUNDS LIKE SOMEONE'S BEEN TO "TITANIC"... AGAIN!

I DON'T CARE WHAT MY FRIENDS SAY — IT'S **JUST** AS SAD THE SIXTH TIME!

WELL, I'VE HEARD THAT.

KIM, CAN I ASK YOU A PERSONAL QUESTION?

SURE, HONEY.

HAVE YOU EVER LOST A LOVER TO HYPO-THERMIA?

HMM... LET ME THINK.

IF ONLY JACK HAD FOUND ANOTHER DOOR TO FLOAT ON! THEN HE AND ROSE COULD HAVE FULFILLED THEIR TRUE DESTINY.

JACK WAS SO GALLANT AND BRAVE AND BEAUTI-FUL. WHY DID HE HAVE TO DIE? I BETTER HAVE A MOMENT OF SILENCE...

UM... ACTUALLY, SWEETHEART, JACK WASN'T A REAL...

HOLD ON. I'M HAVING ANOTHER MOMENT.

HEY, LADIES — WHY THE LONG FACES?

UM... MIKE, THIS IS SORT OF GIRL TALK.

OH... OKAY. SORRY.

>SIGH...<

KIM, DO YOU THINK I'LL EVER FIND SOMEONE AS BEAUTIFUL AS LEO?

I FOUND YOUR FATHER, DIDN'T I?

YOU KNOW THE SADDEST THING ABOUT "TITANIC"? THERE CAN'T BE A SEQUEL!

DO YOU THINK THEY'LL MAKE OTHER GIRL-FRIENDLY, ROMANTIC DISASTER EPICS LIKE "TITANIC"?

I DOUBT IT. THE FILM WAS $100 MILLION OVER BUDGET.

$100 **MILLION**! ARE YOU **KIDDING** ME?

NOPE — THAT'S WHY THEY COULDN'T AFFORD A SCRIPT.

OH... I WONDERED ABOUT THAT.